LAUGH-OUT-LOUD HILARIOUS HALLOWEEN & HORROR HUMOR-666 SPOOK-TACULARLY FUNNY JOKES & SCARY SILLY STORIES OF AUTHOR BIOS

Haunting Ghostly Giggling Guffaws, Creepy CORNY Cackles, Witty Witchy Wickedness

Varius N. Sundry & Miss
A. Laneous

Perfect Publishing

ISBN-13: 9798340879011

Cover design by: Art Painter
Library of Congress Control Number: 2018675309
Printed in the United States of America

CONTENTS

SOME AUTHORS/ ILLUSTRATIONS

All of their hysterical bio-graphical, necro-graffical, autops-illogical stories are postmortem - at the back of this book!

Misty Knight

Spook E. Specter

A whole host of ghost-writers

Bella Luggiles

Anita Body

Mort Tishan

Zed Deadman

Wanda Spell

Wizard of Ahhs

Warren Wolfe

Lycan B. Normal

Furrest Howlington

Mon Starr

INTRODUCTION

Why did the undead

chicken cross the road?

To get to end the fool.

Knock, knock!!

Who's there? ...

The undead chicken

- Unknown undead

1. GHOSTS AND APPARITIONS (HOW TO GHOST ON APPS)

All The Authors' Biography Stories Are At The End....Of This Book

Ghostwritten By Misty Knight

G. Host

Phantom Writer

& Spook E. Specter

Why did the ghost go to therapy?
He had too many haunting memories.

What do ghosts serve for dessert?
Ice scream!

Why did the ghost get lost in the amusement park?
He couldn't find the roller-ghoster.

How do necromancers keep fit?
They do plenty of deadlifts.

What did the ghost say when it found its boo?
"You're the ghoul of my dreams!"

Why are ghosts so bad at telling lies?
Because you can see right through them.

What's a ghost's favorite ride at the fair?
The roller-groaster.

Why did the ghost join a band?
He had great spirit.

How do ghosts send letters?
Through the ghost office.

What's a ghost's favorite fruit?
Boo-berries!

Why did the ghost go to the bar?
For the boos!

What do ghosts wear when it rains?
Boo-ts.

Why are ghosts such bad liars?
Because you can see right through them.

What do you call a ghost's true love?
His ghoul-friend.

Why did the ghost go into the bar?
He was looking for the spirit in the spirits.

How do ghosts send letters?
Through the ghost office.

What kind of street do ghosts haunt?
Dead ends.

Why don't ghosts like rainy weather?
It dampens their spirits.

What did the ghost say to the comedian?
"You boo me away!"

Why do ghosts make good cheerleaders?
Because they have a lot of spirit!

2. VAMPIRES AND DRACULA (YES, THIS CHAPTER REALLY DOES SUCK!)

By Count Pun-Ula

And His Cousin Count Pen-Ula, Dr. Acula & Bella Lugiggles

Why did Dracula become a vegetarian?
He heard stake was bad for his heart.

What's a vampire's favorite ship?
A blood vessel.

Why did the vampire need mouthwash?
Because he had bat breath.

How does Dracula stay fit?
Lots of coffin and running.

What's a vampire's least favorite meal?
Garlic bread.

Why did the vampire take art classes?
He wanted to learn how to draw blood.

What's a vampire's favorite dog?
A bloodhound.

Why are vampires so impulsive?
They never reflect on things.

What did Elvis Dracula say when he was defeated?
"Well, fang you very much!"

How do vampires get around on Halloween?
In blood donation vans

Why did the vampire read the newspaper?
He heard it had great circulation.

What's a vampire's favorite fruit?
Neck-tarines.

Why do vampires need mouthwash?
Because they have bat breath.

How does a vampire start a letter?
"Tomb it may concern..."

Why don't vampires go to the beach?
They're afraid of the sunburn.

What is a vampire's favorite ice cream flavor?
Vein-illa.

Why did the vampire take art class?
He wanted to learn how to draw blood.

How do vampires get around on Halloween?
On blood vessels.

Why are vampires like false teeth?
They come out at night.

What did the vampire say to his sick friend?
"Hope you get bat-ter soon!"

3. ZOMBIES AND THE UNDEAD (AND THE GRATEFULLY DEAD)

By Ray N. Carnation, Sunta B. A. Ghoul,

Anita Rest, Mort Tishen & Zed Deadman

What did the undead Dead Head say when he sobered up?
"This music...sucks!"

Why did the zombie become a DJ?
He loved dropping sick beats.

What's a zombie's favorite toy?
A dead-y bear.

Why did the zombie refuse to eat brains?
He was on a strict die-t.

How do zombies relax after a long day?
They kick back and decompose.

What do zombies wear on their heads?
Brain caps.

Why did the zombie comedian bomb on stage?
His jokes were rotten.

What's a zombie's favorite weather?
Brainstorms.

Why did the zombie go to school?
He wanted to be a no-brainer.

How do zombies celebrate a birthday?
They have a surprise dying party.

Why did the zombie become a chef?
He had a taste for brains cuisine.

Why did the zombie skip school?
He felt rotten.

What do vegetarian zombies eat?
GRAAAINS!

Why did the zombie comedian get booed off stage?
His jokes were dead on arrival.

What's a zombie's favorite exercise?
Dead lifts.

Why did the zombie go to the therapist?
He wanted to work on his dead-ication issues.

How do zombies stay in shape?

They love to jog their memory.

What is a zombie's favorite mode of transportation?
The undead-ground.

Why don't zombies eat clowns?
They taste funny.

What do you call a zombie in a tuxedo?
Dead suave.

Why was the zombie tired?
He had a hard day's fright.

4. WITCHES AND WIZARDS (AND TECHNICAL SUPPORT)

By Wanda Witchful Thinking,

Wanda Spell, Albus Punbledore & Wizard Of Ahhs

Why did the witch enroll in a business class?
She wanted to learn about spell-ing.

What's a wizard's favorite mode of transportation?
A magical staff.

Why did the witch refuse to fly her broom?
She was swept off her feet.

How do wizards clean their teeth?

With tooth spells.

Why did the wizard get lost?
He couldn't find his magic map.

What's a witch's favorite subject?
Hex-ercise.

Why did the wizard bring a ladder to the library?
To reach the top shelf of spell books.

What did the witch say when her potion exploded?
"Well, that's brew-tal!"

Why did the witch open a fast-food restaurant?
She specialized in fast spells.

How do wizards greet each other?
"Spell you later!"

Why don't witches wear flat hats?
There's no point!

What do you call two witches who live together?
Broom-mates.

Why was the witch's broom late?
It over-swept.

What do you call a wizard from outer space?
A flying sorcerer.

Why did the witch enroll in a cooking class?
She wanted to learn new potions.

How does a witch style her hair?
With scare-spray.

What kind of makeup do witches wear?

Ma-scare-a.

Why was the witch kicked out of school?
She couldn't control her spells.

What do you get when you cross a witch with ice?
A cold spell.

Why do wizards clean their teeth three times a day?
To prevent bat breath.

5. WEREWOLVES AND SHAPE-SHIFTERS (AND OUT-OF-SHAPE STICK SHIFTERS)

By Leif N. Shivers,

Warren Wolfe, Lycan B. Normal & Furrest Howlington

What do you call a werewolf with a big vocabulary?
A thesaurus.

Why did the werewolf go to the florist?
He needed some bark for his bite.

How do werewolves prefer their steaks?

Howling hot.

Why was the shape-shifter always late?
He couldn't decide what to wear.

What's a werewolf's favorite musical?
Fur-mione.

Why did the werewolf fail math?
He couldn't handle the wolf-gebra.

What did the werewolf say at the comedy club?
"I'm here all night!"

Why do werewolves make terrible dancers?
They have two left feet.

What do you call a shape-shifter who can't change?
Stuck.

Why did the werewolf take a nap?
He was dog-tired.

Why did the werewolf go to the dressing room?
He was trying on some new fur coats.

What's a werewolf's favorite holiday?
Howl-oween.

Why was the werewolf arrested at the zoo?
He was found moonlighting.

What do you call a werewolf who's feeling under the weather?
Ailing at the moon.

Why don't werewolves ever know the time?
Because they're always howling at the wrong time.

What happened when the werewolf swallowed a clock?
He got ticks.

How do you stop a werewolf from attacking?
Throw a stick and yell "Fetch!"

Why did the shape-shifter fail art class?
He kept changing his medium.

What do you call a werewolf with no legs?
Anything you like, he can't chase you.

Why was the werewolf sad?
He had a ruff day.

6. MONSTERS AND CREATURES (KIDS!)

By Frank N. Stein (Seen Here At His Day Job: Selling Hot Dogs And Beer) ,

Beastly Writerson & Mon Starr

Why did the monster eat a light bulb?
He wanted a light snack.

What's a monster's favorite game?
Hide and shriek.

Why did the monster join the choir?
He had a monstrous voice.

What do you call a polite monster?
A civil ogre.

Why did the monster bring a ladder to school?
To reach new heights.

What's a monster's favorite dessert?
Boonana split.

Why did the monster sit under the tree?
He was waiting for his ghoul-friend.

What do monsters read before bed?
Horror-scopes.

Why did the monster refuse to eat fast food?
It gave him indigestion.

How do monsters tell their future?
They use a crystal beast.

Why don't monsters eat ghosts?
They taste like sheet.

What do sea monsters eat?
Fish and ships.

Why was the monster good at math?
He wasn't afraid to count Dracula.

What's a monster's favorite play?
Romeo and Ghouliet.

How do monsters like their eggs?
Terror-fried.

Why did the monster's mother knit him three socks?
She heard he grew another foot.

What do you call a friendly monster?

A good fiend.

Why do monsters make good dancers?
They have all the right moves.

What kind of music do monsters listen to?
Heavy metal.

Why did the monster eat a light bulb?
Because he wanted a light snack.

7. HAUNTED HOUSES (IN HILARIOUS HILL AREAS)

By Manor O. Fear, Haunt E. Mansion & Johnny N. Shining

What's a haunted house's favorite TV show?
"Ghost Whisperer."

Why did the ghost throw a party in the haunted house?
To raise some spirits.

What did the realtor say about the haunted house?
"It has great curb ape-peal!"

Why did the haunted house feel cold?
It was full of drafts.

How do you make a haunted house less scary?

Add some boo-kay flowers.

What did the ghost use to repair his haunted house?
Spook-tacular tools.

Why did the haunted house go to therapy?
It had too many internal conflicts.

What's the favorite food of a haunted house?
Spook-etti.

Why did the skeleton move into the haunted house?
It had lots of closet space.

How does a haunted house write emails?
With ghost-writing software.

Why did the ghost refuse to haunt the house?
It was too drafty.

What do you call a haunted house that sells spirits?
A booze house.

Why did the real estate agent love selling haunted houses?
Great turnover.

What did the owner say when his haunted house didn't sell?
"I guess the spirits aren't interested."

Why was the haunted house so messy?
The ghosts were terrible at housekeeping.

What do you find on a haunted beach?
A sand-witch house.

Why do haunted houses make good retirement homes?
Lots of resident spirits.

What kind of horses do ghosts ride?
Nightmares.

Why was the haunted house self-conscious?
It had too many skeletons in its closet.

What do you call a haunted house with a pool?
A scare-B&B.

8. SKELETONS AND BONES (KEEP 'EM IN THE CLOSET...AND SMOKE 'EM)

By Dustin Bones, Skel E. Ton,
Anita Body & Cal C. Um

Why did the skeleton go to the BBQ?
To get some spare ribs.

What did the skeleton say when he rode his motorcycle?
"Bone to be wild!"

Why was the skeleton comedian so popular?
He had a funny bone.

How did the skeleton know it was going to rain?
He could feel it in his bones.

What's a skeleton's favorite drink?
Milk—it's good for the bones.

Why did the skeleton study in the graveyard?
He wanted a higher bone-ification.

What did the doctor say to the skeleton?
"This will tickle a little."

Why are skeletons always so calm?
Nothing gets under their skin.

What do you call a skeleton snake?
A rattler.

How do skeletons send secret messages?
In rig a mortis-code.

Why didn't the skeleton go to the party?
He had no body to go with.

Why are skeletons so calm?
Nothing gets under their skin.

What do you call a skeleton who won't work?
Lazy bones.

Why did the skeleton cross the road?
To get to the body shop.

What instrument do skeletons play?
The trombone.

Why didn't the skeleton laugh at the joke?
He didn't find it humerus.

What do you call a skeleton who tells jokes?
A funny bone.

Why was the skeleton afraid of the storm?
He didn't have any guts.

How do skeletons call their friends?

On the tele-bone.

What do skeletons say before they begin dining?
Bone appetit!

9. MUMMIES AND ANCIENT CURSES (MY MOM?: "DARN IT!")

By Pharaoh Moans, Wrapsody Jones & Annie Tut

Why did the mummy go on a diet?
He wanted to keep his wraps slim.

What did the mummy say when he was invited to dinner?
"That would be de-lightful!"

Why was the mummy such a good listener?
He was all ears.

What's a mummy's favorite kind of coffee?
De-coffin-ated.

Why did the mummy open a bakery?
He was great at making wrap sandwiches.

How do mummies keep their hair in place?
With scare-spray.

Why was the mummy comedian so bad?
His jokes were ancient.

What's a mummy's favorite flower?
Chrysanthemummies.

Why did the mummy get promoted?
He was an up-and-comer.

What's a mummy's favorite instrument?
The tomb-a.

Why don't mummies take vacations?
They're afraid they'll relax and unwind.

What is a mummy's favorite kind of music?
Wrap music.

Why was the mummy anxious?
He was all wound up.

What did the mummy say to the detective?
"Let's wrap this up."

Why did the mummy get a promotion?
He was an asset to the company.

Why do mummies have trouble keeping friends?
They're too clingy.

What kind of coffee do mummies drink?
De-coffin-ated.

Why was the mummy comedian a flop?
His jokes fell flat.

What did the ancient curse say to the explorer?
"You're doomed, but have a nice day!"

Why do mummies make excellent spies?
They're good at keeping things under wraps.

10. PUMPKINS AND JACK-O'-LANTERNS (ALWAYS SMILING? ALWAYS LAUGHING?)

By Jack O. Lantern, Gord N. Orange & Autumn Carver

Why did the pumpkin join the rock band?
He had a smashing pumpkin personality.

What did the pumpkin say to his carver?
"You light up my life!"

Why was the pumpkin so forgetful?
Because he was empty-headed.

What do you call a pumpkin that works at the beach?
A life-gourd.

Why did the pumpkin bring a book to the party?
He was told to bring some pulp fiction.

What's a pumpkin's favorite genre?
Gourd-geous romance.

Why did the pumpkin turn green?

It was feeling a little sick o' lantern.

What's a pumpkin's favorite sport?
Gourd games.

Why was the Jack-o'-lantern afraid of heights?
He was a little light-headed.

What did the scientist say to the pumpkin?
"You've got potential, let's carve out your future!"

Why was the Jack-o'-lantern afraid to cross the road?
It had no guts.

What do you get when you drop a pumpkin?
Squash.

Why was the pumpkin late for the meeting?
It got stuck in a jam.

How do you fix a broken pumpkin?
With a pumpkin patch.

Why did the pumpkin turn red?
Because it saw the salad dressing.

What did the pumpkin say to the carver?
"Cut it out!"

Why do pumpkins sit on people's porches?
They have no hands to knock on the door.

What did one Jack-o'-lantern say to the other on the way to the party?
"Let's get glowing!"

What is a pumpkin's favorite sport?
Squash.

Why did the pumpkin cross the road?

To get to the pumpkin patch.

11. BLACK CATS AND SUPERSTITIONS (STEVIE!!)

By Felix Omen, Kitty K. Lure & Whiskers Mcluck

Why do black cats never get lost?
They always find their way meow-t.

What did the black cat say after a big meal?
"I'm feline fine!"

Why did the black cat avoid mirrors?
He didn't want to risk bad luck.

What do black cats like to eat on hot days?
Mice cream.

Why are black cats good at video games?
They have nine lives.

What's a black cat's favorite color?
Purr-ple.

Why did the black cat sit on the mat?
To catch the morning mews.

What did the superstitious person say when he saw a black cat?

"Guess I'm in fur a treat!"
Why did the black cat start a band?

He had great mew-sical talent.
How do black cats celebrate Halloween?

They throw a cat-tastic party.Why don't black cats play poker in the jungle?
Too many cheetahs.

What did the black cat say after making a mistake?
"You've got to be kitten me!"

Why was the black cat so good at video games?
He had nine lives.

Why did the black cat sit on the computer?
To keep an eye on the mouse.

What happens when a black cat falls off a broomstick?
He witch-hikes home.

Why are black cats bad at storytelling?
They only have one tale.

What do you call it when a black cat wins a dog show?
A catastrophe.

Why did the black cat avoid the mirror?
It was afraid of seven years of bad luck.

Why was the black cat a great singer?
Because it was very mewsical.

What did the superstitious man say when he saw a black cat?
"Looks like I'm feline lucky today!"

12. GRAVEYARDS AND TOMBSTONES (I'D RATHER PASS... GALLSTONES!)

By Phil Graves, Doug M. Deep & Hughes Mort Stone

Why did the vampire subscribe to the newspaper?
He heard there were grave reviews.

Why are graveyards always over-crowded?
People arc always dying to get in.

What's a ghost's favorite dessert?
Boo-berry pie.

Why did the skeleton go to the graveyard?
He was bone to be wild.

What's a vampire's favorite part of the graveyard?
The necks tomb over.

Why are graveyards so noisy?
Because of all the coffin.

How do ghosts like their steak?
Medium scare.

What did one tombstone say to the other?
"I'm dying to tell you something!"

Why did the zombie get lost in the graveyard?
He couldn't find his plot.

What's the most popular genre in the graveyard library?
Mystery—everyone loves a good who-died-it.

Why did the ghost bring a ladder to the graveyard?
To reach the high spirits.

What's a graveyard's favorite game?
Hide and shriek.

What did one tombstone say to the other?
"Isn't life grave?"

Why was the graveyard so noisy?
Because of all the coffin.

What kind of jokes do you tell in a graveyard?
Tombstones.

Why did the skeleton bring a ladder to the graveyard?
To reach the high spirits.

What do you call a party in a graveyard?
A tomb-munity gathering.

Why are graveyards so popular?
People are just dying to get there.

What did the ghost find when he went to the library?
Lots of grave books.

Why did the zombie avoid the graveyard?
He didn't have the guts to go back.

13. SPOOKY SOUNDS AND NOISES (MESSAGES FROM URANUS)

By Echo Howl, Whis Per Wind & Cree Key Door

What do ghosts use to make music?
Sheet music.

What do you call a spooky noise that scares chickens?
A poultry-geist.

Why did the spooky sound feel lonely?
Because everyone ghosted it.

What's a ghost's favorite musical instrument?
The boo-kulele.

Why did the haunted house make weird noises?
It was the ghost's jam session.

How do you know when a ghost is sad?
It lets out a boo-hoo.

What's a skeleton's favorite song?
"Bad to the Bone."

Why did the witch's cauldron sound off-key?
It was brewing a flat note.

What noise does a witch's car make?
"Broom broom!"

Why was the werewolf's howl off-key?
He had a sore throat.

How do bats communicate?
Through echolol-cation.

What do you call a noisy vampire?
A hemogoblin.

Why was the ghost musician so bad?
He didn't have any soul.

What sound do witches make when they eat cereal?
Snap, cackle, and pop.

Why was the ghost musician so famous?
He had haunting melodies.

What did one spooky sound say to the other?
"Do you come here often, or am I just hearing things?"

What instrument does a skeleton play?
The xylobone.

Why did the door creak?
Because it had a spooky hinge.

Why did the spooky noise win an award?
It was outstanding in its field.

14. FULL MOONS AND NIGHTTIME (BEST TIME TO HANG 'EM!)

By Luna Tick, Stella Knight & N. Somnia

Why did the werewolf go to art school?
He wanted to learn lunar drawing.

What do you call a crazy moon?
A lunatic.

Why did the man refuse to go outside during a full moon?
He was afraid of moonstruck cows.
How does the moon get his hair done?
Eclipse it.

What's a vampire's favorite time of day?
Nighty-night.
Why did the astronaut throw a party on the moon?
Because it had great space.

What do you call an argument on the moon?
A lunar-tic attack.

Why was the night sad?

Because it didn't get any stars.

How do you organize a party in space?
You planet.

Why did the moon skip dinner?
It was full.

Why did the werewolf stay indoors during the full moon?
He was moon-bathing.

What do you call a nighttime gardener?
A meteor.

Why did the owl invite his friends over?
For a hootenanny.

Why is the moon so broke?
Because it's down to its last quarter.

What did the moon say to his therapist?
"I'm just going through a phase."

Why do wolves howl at the moon?
Because there always hungry and it looks like a giant scoop of ice scream

How does the man in the moon cut his hair?
Eclipse it.

Why wouldn't the moon eat it's dinner?
It was a full moon.

What did the star say to the moon?
"You light up my night."

Why did the vampire admire the night sky...over Hollywood?
He loved star-grazing.

15. TRICK-OR-TREATING ADVENTURES (SMELL MY FEET?)

By Candy Cornwell, Treat A. Lot & Dora Belle

Why did the skeleton go trick-or-treating at a barbecue?
To get some spare ribs.

What's a ghost's favorite candy?
Boo-ble gum.

Why did the kid dress up as a computer for Halloween?
To get some megabites.

What candy do vampires refuse to eat?
Lifesavers.

Why did the witch refuse to wear a flat hat?
There was no point.

What did the vampire, Robert Hopeless, say after trick-or-treating?
"Fangs for the memories!"

Why did the singing pirate bring a ladder trick-or-treating?
To reach the high seas (C's).

How do monsters tell their fortunes on Halloween?
Through their horror-scopes.

Why did the ghost refuse to trick-or-treat?
He had no-body to go with.

What's a mummy's favorite type of music while trick-or-treating?
Wrap music.

Why did the kid dress up as a candy bar for Halloween?
So he could have one extra treat!

What do you call a bee that can't make up its mind which candy to take while trick-or-treating on Halloween?
A maybee.

Why did the skeleton refuse to go knocking on strange doors for trick-or-treating?
He didn't have the guts.

What do birds say on Halloween?
"Trick or tweet!"

Why did the vampire take an art class before Halloween?
He wanted to learn how to draw blood.

What do you get when you divide the circumference of a Jack-o'-lantern by its diameter?
Pumpkin Pi.

Why was the broom late for trick-or-treating?
It over-swept.

What kind of music do mummies listen to while trick-or-treating?

Wrap music.

Why did the ghost pick his own candy?
He had no body to do it for him.

What do you call a ghost's true love?
His ghoul-friend.

16. COSTUME MISHAPS (WHOOOOPSIES!)

By Ward Robe Malfunction, Zowie Button & Z. Pear Gone

Why did the mummy's costume fall apart?
He ran out of toilet paper.

What happened when the vampire couldn't find his cape?
He couldn't turn into a bat or fly away...just wasn't cape-able

Why did the kid's vampire costume fail?
He couldn't find his cape-abilities.

What happened when the witch tried to fix her broken broom?

She realized she couldn't handle it.

Why did the ghost's costume look so cheap?
He got it on a skeleton budget.

What did Frankenstein say when he couldn't find a costume?
"Guess I'll have to wing it!"

Why did the zombie's costume fall apart?
It was dead on arrival.

How did the mummy feel when his costume unraveled?
Totally wrapped up in the moment.

Why was the werewolf's costume too tight?
He didn't account for fur shrinkage.

What did the pumpkin say when its costume didn't fit?
"I guess I'm out of my gourd!"

Why did the alien's costume get disqualified?
It was too far out.

What did the skeleton say when he couldn't find a costume?
"I'm bone dry on ideas!"

Why was the ghost's costume so wrinkled?
He couldn't find his iron (...chains!?...)

Why did the skeleton have to stay home?
Too many had bones to pick with him

What do you call it when someone dresses as a cloud and it rains?
A costume malfunction.

Why did the pumpkin costume quit?
It couldn't keep its head on straight.

What did the boy say when he realized his costume was too tight?
"I think I've created a monster!"

Why did the witch have to cancel her costume party?
Her wardrobe had a spell on it.

What happened when the werewolf's costume ripped?
He was fur-ious.

Why did the zombie refuse to wear his costume?

It didn't have enough *brains*.

17. MAGIC SPELLS AND POTIONS (MAGIC SPELLS...BECAUSE I CAN'T...#9?)

By Al K. Mist, Potion Ivy & Brewster Spellman

Why did the witch get kicked out of school?
She couldn't spell.

Why did the witch use GPS?
She didn't want to have (t)a spell "lost".

What do you call a potion that makes you disappear?
Evapor-ate.
Why was the wizard good at cooking?
He knew how to stir up magic.

How do witches stay positive?
They use affirmations.

What did the apprentice wizard say to his mentor?
"You're the wand that I want!"

Why did the witch fail her potion exam?
She couldn't concentrate.

What's a wizard's favorite dance move?
The spell shuffle.

Why did the wizard start recycling?
He wanted to reduce, reuse, re-magic.

What do you call a magician on a plane?
A flying sorcerer.

How does a witch write in her diary?
In cursive.

What do you call an unpredictable potion?
A loose cannon.

Why was the wizard's potion shop failing?
He couldn't find the right mix.

What did the wizard say when his potion exploded?
"Well, that's a brew-tal outcome."

Why did the magic spell fail?
It was spell-checked.

What do witches put on to go trick-or-treating?
Mas-scare-a.

How do you make a witch itch?
Take away the 'w'.

What do you get when you cross a snowman and a wizard?
Frostbite.

Why did the witch switch to decaf?
Too many restless nights stirring.

What did the apprentice say after a successful spell?
"That's wand-erful!"

18. SCARECROWS AND CORNFIELDS (IN CORNY, HILLARIOUS HILL AREAS)

By Cornelius Crow, Hayden Fields & Scary Crowley

Why did the scarecrow win an award?
Because he was outstanding in his field.

What did the cornfield say when it got scared?
"Aw, shucks!"

Why don't scarecrows eat much?
They're already stuffed.

Why did the scarecrow keep getting promoted?
He was outstanding in his field.
(I would have gotten that one - I heard it before - if I only had a brain!!)

What's a scarecrow's favorite fruit?
Straw-berries.

Why did the scarecrow win the Nobel Prize?
For being out-standing in his field.
(...if I only had a brain!)

What do you call a scarecrow with lots of awards?
A straw-studded celebrity.

Why did the scarecrow fail at stand-up comedy?
His jokes were too corny.

How do scarecrows drink their cocktails?
With a straw.

Why did the scarecrow go broke?
Because he couldn't keep his crows in a row.

What's a scarecrow's favorite sport?
Hay-kido.

Why did the scarecrow get a promotion?
He was outstanding in his field—again!

How do you make a scarecrow happy?
Just say hay.

What do you call a scarecrow with a PhD?

Doctor of Scare-iculture.

Why was the scarecrow promoted?
He was the straw boss.

Why did the scarecrow join the debate team?
He was a great straw man.

How do scarecrows greet each other?
"Hay there!"

Why was the cornfield haunted?
It had stalkers.

What did the farmer say to the mischievous scarecrow?
"You're pushing my buttons!"

Why did the scarecrow refuse to go to the Halloween party?
He didn't have the guts to socialize.

19. BATS AND NOCTURNAL CREATURES (TURN N KNOCK 'EM OUT...THEY'RE...BATTY...)

By Batty Knight, Batty Day Vis, Owl F. T. R. Hours & Ben N. Darkness

Why do bats sleep during the day?
So they can hang out all night.

What did the bat say to his friend when they got lost?
"Let's wing it!"

Why did the bat miss school?
He was hanging out at home.

What do you call a bat in a belfry?
A dingbat.

Why are bats so good at baseball?
They're naturals with bats.

What's a bat's favorite place to shop?
The bat-mall.

Why did the bat go to the doctor?
He had the bat-teries.

What do you get when you cross a bat and a computer?
Love at first byte.

Why did the owl invite the bat to his party?
Because he was a hoot.

What's a bat's favorite movie?
"Bat to the Future."

How do bats freshen their breath?
With bat mints.

Why did the bat become a lawyer?
He was good at winging it.

Why don't bats live alone?
They like to hang with their friends.

What's a bat's favorite dessert?
I-Scream.

Why did the bat miss the party?
He couldn't find the right flight path.

What do you call a bat in a belfry?
A dingbat.

Why did the bat need a tutor?
He was having trouble with his echolocation.

What do you get when you cross a bat with a laptop?

Love at first byte.

Why did the nocturnal creature bring a ladder?
To see the dark side of the moon.

What do bats say when they return to the roost?
"Home, tweet home!"

20. ALIEN ENCOUNTERS AND UFOS (IT KEPT GETTING BIGGER...THEN... IT HIT ME)

By Al E. N., Martian Wells & U.f. Owen

Why did the alien get a parking ticket?
He forgot to pay the parking meteor.

What do aliens serve their tea in?
Flying saucers.

Why did the alien join a band?
He wanted to make some space jams.

Why did the alien go to the restaurant?
He wanted a taste that was out of this world.

What do aliens say when they land on Earth?
"Take me to your dealer!"

Why was the alien so light-hearted?
He had a good sense of humors.

What do you call an alien with no eyes?
An al_n.

Why did the alien fail math?
He couldn't grasp Earth's gravity.

How do aliens pay for coffee?
With star-bucks.

Why did the alien become a gardener?
He had a green thumb.

What's an alien's favorite key on the keyboard?
The space bar.

Why did the alien bring a ladder to the bar?
Because the drinks were out of this world.

What do you call an alien spaceship that goes nowhere?
A UFO—Unidentified Floating Object.

What do you call an alien with three eyes?
An aliiien.

Why are aliens so smart?
They're always looking for intelligent life.

What did one UFO say to the other?
"I'm just here for the atmosphere."

Why did the alien fail the test?
He didn't planet well.

How do aliens organize a party?

They planet.

What do aliens like to read?
Comet books.

Why did the alien go to the doctor?
He had a flying saucer stomach.

Mid-Book Review Request Page

(The Entire Rest of the Book Continues After This Brief Request!)

SHARE A CHUCKLE, MAKE A DIFFERENCE!

Spread The Laughter (It's Contagious But In A Good Way!)

"Laughter is the best medicine, and it's also calorie-free!" – Count Chuckula

Hey there, fellow joke lover! You've already made it halfway through this crazy, spooky, and downright hilarious journey with **"Laugh-Out-Loud Hilarious Halloween & Horror Humor: 666 Spook-tacularly Funny Jokes & Spooky Silly Stories of Authors' Biographies."** Are your sides aching yet? Have you snorted milk out of your nose at least once? (If not, keep reading!)

Now, imagine if you could share that joy with someone else. Yep, it's easier than handing out candy on Halloween night!

Would you be willing to help out another joke-loving ghoul who's on the hunt for something monstrously funny to read? By leaving a review, you'll be guiding others to a treasure chest full of giggles, cackles, and belly laughs.

Why does it matter? Well, most people pick books based on reviews. That means your opinion could be the deciding factor in making someone's day a little brighter, their night a little spookier, and their bookshelf a whole lot funnier.

And guess what? It's free, takes less than a minute, and might just help...

- •...one more kid tell the perfect joke at their school's Halloween party.
- •...one more person find something to smile about after a rough day.
- •...one more monster under the bed learn to laugh instead of growl!

So, if you've enjoyed this wild, wacky ride so far, I'd be thrilled if you'd share your thoughts. Just scan the spooky QR code below and leave your review—it's easier than finding your way out of a haunted house!

Aim any smartphone camera at the Black and White Q R Code above and click OK to go to the link to review: Laugh Out Loud Hilrious Halloween & Horror Humor

Or please, try copying or clicking on the link below:

https://www.amazon.com/review/review-your-purchases/?

asin=B0DJ9NB2NG

OR: Please, go to   www.Amazon.com   and search for this title in order to leave a review. We cannot possibly thank you enough!!

If you're the kind of person who loves to share a good laugh, then you're absolutely my kind of people! Thank you from the bottom of my not-so-scary heart!

Your Gratefully Undead Comedian,

Varius N. Sundry - with Miss A. Laneous & the Rest of the Team (RIP!!)

Please, keep reading - it only gets better!

HERE ARE 200 ABSOLUTELY HILARIOUS, FUNNY, AND LAUGH-OUT-LOUD JOKES CATEGORIZED ACROSS A VARIETY OF HALLOWEEN, HORROR, SPOOKY, AND CREEPY THEMES.

Whether you're hosting a party, sharing with friends, or just enjoying some seasonal humor, these jokes are sure to de-light!

1. GENERAL HALLOWEEN HUMOR (GOOD HUMOR...MAN, THE GENERAL OF I SCREAM!)

1. **Why don't mummies take vacations?**

   They're afraid they'll unwind.
2. **What do you call a cleaning skeleton?**

   The grim sweeper.
3. **Why didn't the ghost go to the party?**

   He had no body to dance with.
4. **What's a vampire's favorite ice cream flavor?**

   Vein-illa.
5. **Why do witches not get along with baseball players?**

   Because they keep stealing their bats.
6. **What do you get when you cross a pumpkin with a spider?**

   A pumpkin web.

7. **Why did the scarecrow win an award?**

Because he was outstanding in his field.

8. **What do you call two witches sharing an apartment?**

Broommates.

9. **Why don't ghosts like rain?**

It dampens their spirits.

10. **What type of dog does Dracula have?**

A bloodhound.

---

2. GOTHIC ROMANCE GIGGLES ('N' COOTIES!!)

11. Why did the vampire read the newspaper?

He heard it had great circulation.

12. What did the gothic romance novelist say to her vampire lover?

"You make my heart race faster than a bat out of hell."

13. Why did the ghost refuse to date the vampire?

He couldn't see a future together.

14. What's a gothic lover's favorite flower?

A black rose.

15. Why did the werewolf break up with his gothic girlfriend?

She was too hound-damental.

16. What do you call a romantic dinner for monsters?

A frightful feast.

17. Why did the gothic poet bring a candle to the séance?

To light up his dark verses.

18. What's a vampire's favorite romantic movie?

Pride and Prey-judice.

19. Why did the ghost write a love letter?

He wanted to express his undying love.

20. How do gothic romances end?

With a happy haunting.

---

3. CREEPY LEGENDS LAUGHS (AT YOUR ATTEMPT TO...FLEE)

21. **Why did the legend of the Loch Ness Monster apply for a job?**

    It wanted to prove it's not just a myth.

22. **What do you call a legendary creature that tells jokes?**

    A chuckle-ichthyosaurus.

23. **Why don't legends ever get lost?**

    They always have a mythical map.

24. **What's a legendary creature's favorite game?**

    Hide and shriek.

25. **Why did the Bigfoot start a comedy club?**

    To share his hairy jokes.

26. **How do legends stay in shape?**

    They do ghost runs.

27. **Why was the Yeti a bad comedian?**

    His jokes were too cold.

28. **What's a legend's favorite type of music?**

    Rock and folklore.

29. **Why did the vampire join the legends' comedy troupe?**

He wanted to suck the seriousness out of life.

30. **What do you call a legendary creature who loves puns?**

A pun-osaur.

4. FRIGHTENING FOLKLORE FUNNIES (WHY THEY DIED...ONSTAGE)

31. **Why did the folklore character bring a ladder to the bar?**

    To reach the high spirits.

32. **What do you call folklore stories about funny monsters?**

    Tall tales with a twist.

33. **Why did the bogeyman apply for a stand-up gig?**

    He wanted to scare up some laughs.

34. **How does folklore keep its traditions alive?**

    Through eerie storytelling.

35. **Why don't folklore creatures use social media?**

    They prefer to keep things under wraps.

36. **What's a folklore hero's favorite dessert?**

    Hero-cakes.

37. **Why was the witch's broom late to the folklore meeting?**

    It over-swept.

38. **What do you call a folklore character who tells jokes while fishing?**

A pun-isher.

39. Why did the ghost enroll in folklore studies?

To improve his haunting techniques.

40. How do folklore creatures stay organized?

They use spooky planners.

5. SPOOKY MOVIE MIRTH (HOLLYWOOD IS BECOMING A...JOKE)

41. **Why did the zombie refuse to watch horror movies?**

   He found them too brainless.

42. **What's a ghost's favorite movie genre?**

   Spook-tacular thrillers.

43. **Why did the vampire director hire only night owls?**

   To keep the set lively after dark.

44. **What do you call a comedy horror film about clowns?**

   Jester Fright.

45. **Why did the werewolf get a role in the horror movie?**

   He was a natural howl-star.

46. **What's a mummy's favorite scene in a movie?**

   The wrap-up.

47. **Why don't witches make good movie stars?**

   They always wing it.

48. **What do you call a romantic horror film?**

Love Bites.

49. Why did the haunted house become a film set?

It had all the right props.

50. What's a ghost's favorite part of making movies?

The boo-ming lights.

6. SCARY STORY SNICKERS (HANGRY?)

51. Why did the storyteller bring a ladder to the campfire?

To reach new heights in storytelling.

52. What's a ghost's favorite bedtime story?

The Very Frightening Caterpillar.

53. Why don't scary stories ever get cold?

Because they always have chilling details.

54. What do you call a scary story about vegetables?

The Tale of the Killer Kale.

55. Why did the monster love writing scary stories?

He enjoyed the suspense.

56. What's a ghost's favorite scary story trope?

The unexpected twist.

57. Why was the vampire's scary story so popular?

It had bite.

58. How do scary stories stay fit?

They do spine twists.

59. Why did the witch write a scary story?

To cast a spell of fear and laughter.

60. What's a skeleton's favorite scary story?

The Haunting of Bone Manor.

7. SPOOKY SOUND EFFECTS (MORE MESSAGES FROM BEYOND... URANUS)

61. Why did the ghost start a band?

He had great spirit.

62. What's a witch's favorite sound?

The hiss-terical laughter.

63. Why do vampires love classical music?

Because of the bat-tatas.

64. What do you call a noisy skeleton?

Rattle-taylor.

65. Why was the haunted house so musical?

It had plenty of ghost notes.

66. What sound does a mummy make when he laughs?

Wrap-r!

67. Why do werewolves love loud music?

It helps them howl in harmony.

68. What's a ghost's favorite instrument?

The boos-tonica.

69. Why did the monster join the orchestra?

He wanted to play the beast-ly trumpet.

70. What sound does a haunted piano make?

Booo-gehmoody.

---

8. FRIGHTENING FOOD FUNNIES (FAMISHED...OR AMISHED?)

71. **Why did the ghost eat a light bulb?**

    He wanted a light snack.

72. **What do vampires eat for breakfast?**

    A Bloody Mary.

73. **Why don't mummies eat fast food?**

    They prefer something wrap-turous.

74. **What's a zombie's favorite restaurant?**

    IHOP—for the brains.

75. **Why did the witch bring a ladder to the kitchen?**

    To reach the high spirits in her potions.

76. **What do werewolves order at a steakhouse?**

    Rare steaks, howling medium, and well-done.

77. **Why did the skeleton refuse dessert?**

    He had no stomach for sweets.

78. **What's a ghost's favorite fruit?**

Boo-berries.

79. Why did the vampire start a bakery?

To make blood-orange muffins.

80. What do you call a haunted cafeteria?

The spooky slammer.

9. CREEPY CREATURE QUIPS (KIDS KIDDING)

81. Why did the Bigfoot apply for a job at the circus?

He wanted to be the main scare.

82. What do you call a friendly monster?

A good fiend.

83. Why was the Yeti always calm?

He knew how to keep his cool in the mountains.

84. What's a mermaid's favorite comedy show?

SpongeBob SquarePants—she loves the underwater humor.

85. Why don't goblins ever get lost?

They follow the mischief maps.

86. What do you call a talking ghost?

A chatty apparition.

87. Why did the Kraken join a band?

He wanted to play the tentacle-ly drums.

88. What's a werewolf's favorite type of humor?

Howling good jokes.

89. Why did the vampire take up gardening?

He wanted to grow his own blood-red roses.

90. What do you call a mythical creature that loves to joke?

A laugh-dragon.

---

10. HAUNTED HOUSE HILARITY (NO BODIES HOME)

91. Why did the haunted house go to school?

To improve its ghost-ucation.

92. What's a haunted house's favorite workout?

Dead lifts.

93. Why did the ghost become a real estate agent?

He knows all about spooky properties.

94. What do you call a haunted house that tells jokes?

A laugh-ment home.

95. Why was the haunted house so good at parties?

It always had the best spirits.

96. How do haunted houses stay cool in the summer?

With lots of eerie air conditioning.

97. What's a haunted house's favorite board game?

Clue—because it loves mysterious things.

98. Why did the haunted house apply for a loan?

To renovate its ghostly features.

99. What do you call a haunted house that's also a bakery?

Spook-etti shop.

100. Why did the haunted house refuse to share its secrets?

It had too many locked rooms.

11. SKELETON AND BONE LAUGHS (ON A BARE-BONES, SKELETAL BUDGET)

101. **Why did the skeleton go to the dance alone?**

    He had no body to go with.

102. **What do you call a skeleton who won't work?**

    Lazy bones.

103. **Why didn't the skeleton fight the zombie?**

    He didn't have the guts.

104. **What do you call a skeleton that tells jokes?**

    A funny bone.

105. **Why do skeletons hate winter?**

    They can't handle the chill in their bones.

106. **How do skeletons call each other?**

    On the tele-bone.

107. **What's a skeleton's favorite instrument?**

    The trom-bone.

108. **Why did the skeleton go to the party?**

To bone up on his social skills.

109. **What type of art do skeletons enjoy?**

Skullptures.

110. **Why are skeletons so calm?**

Nothing gets under their skin.

12. MUMMY AND ANCIENT CURSE COMEDY ("WHAT THE H___ ARE YOU KIDS DOING?")

111. Why did the mummy go on a diet?

He wanted to keep his wraps slim.

112. What do mummies eat for dessert?

Wrap-pies.

113. Why was the mummy a bad comedian?

His jokes were too wrapped up.

114. How do mummies keep their hair in place?

With scare-spray.

115. Why did the mummy enroll in school?

To brush up on his ancient history.

116. What's a mummy's favorite type of music?

Wrap music.

117. Why don't mummies take breaks?

They can't unwind.

118. What did the mummy say to the detective?

"Let's wrap this up."

119. Why did the mummy get promoted?

He was an asset to the company.

120. How do mummies stay warm in the winter?

They bundle up in their layers.

13. PUMPKIN AND JACK-O'-LANTERN JOKES (ONLY FUNNY IF YOU ARE...SMASHED)

121. **Why was the Jack-o'-lantern afraid to cross the road?**

It had no guts.

122. **What do you get when you drop a pumpkin?**

Squash.

123. **Why did the pumpkin turn red?**

Because it saw the salad dressing.

124. **How do you fix a broken pumpkin?**

With a pumpkin patch.

125. **What's a pumpkin's favorite sport?**

Squash.

126. **Why did the pumpkin join the band?**

He had a smashing personality.

127. **What did the pumpkin say to the carver?**

"Cut it out!"

128. Why do pumpkins sit on porches?

They have no hands to knock on the door.

129. What's a pumpkin's favorite place to go?

The gourd-geous gardens.

130. Why did the pumpkin cross the road?

To get to the pumpkin patch.

14. BLACK CATS AND SUPERSTITION SNICKERS (HANGRY STEVIE!!)

131. Why don't black cats play poker in the jungle?

Too many cheetahs.

132. What did the black cat say after making a mistake?

"You've got to be kitten me!"

133. Why was the black cat so good at video games?

He had nine lives.

134. Why did the black cat sit on the computer?

To keep an eye on the mouse.

135. What happens when a black cat falls off a broomstick?

He witch-hikes home.

136. Why are black cats bad at storytelling?

They only have one tale.

137. What do you call it when a black cat wins a dog show?

A catastrophe.

138. Why did the black cat avoid the mirror?

It was afraid of seven years of bad luck.

139. **Why was the black cat a great singer?**

Because it was very mewsical.

140. **What did the superstitious man say when he saw a black cat?**

"Looks like I'm feline lucky today!"

15. GRAVEYARD AND TOMBSTONE GIGGLES (NOT ALL HILARIOUS BUT BETTER THAN BEING BURIED ALIVE...!)

141. Why don't graveyards ever get crowded?

People are always dying to get in.

142. What did one tombstone say to the other?

"Isn't life grave?"

143. Why was the graveyard so noisy?

Because of all the coffin.

144. What kind of jokes do you tell in a graveyard?

Tombstones.

145. Why did the skeleton bring a ladder to the graveyard?

To reach the high spirits.

146. What do you call a party in a graveyard?

A tomb-munity gathering.

147. **Why are graveyards so popular?**

People are just dying to get there.

148. **What did the ghost find when he went to the library?**

Lots of grave books.

149. **Why did the zombie avoid the graveyard?**

He didn't have the guts to go back.

150. **What's a graveyard's favorite game?**

Hide and shriek.

16. SPOOKY SOUND EFFECTS SILLIES (DEAD... SILENCE... CRICKETS...)

151. **What do ghosts use to make music?**

Sheet music.

152. **Why did the noise complain about its job?**

It found it unsettling.

153. **What do you call a spooky noise that scares chickens?**

A poultry-geist.

154. **Why did the spooky sound feel lonely?**

Because everyone ghosted it.

155. **What sound do witches make when they eat cereal?**

Snap, cackle, and pop.

156. **Why was the ghost musician so famous?**

He had haunting melodies.

157. **What did one spooky sound say to the other?**

"Do you come here often, or am I just hearing things?"

158. **Why did the spooky noise win an award?**

It was outstanding in its field.

159. What instrument does a skeleton play?

The xylobone.

160. Why did the door creak?

Because it had a spooky hinge.

17. FULL MOON AND NIGHTTIME NONSENSE (A LITTLE BIT...LOONIE)

161. **Why did the werewolf go to art school?**

   He wanted to learn lunar drawing.

162. **What do you call a crazy moon?**

   A lunatic.

163. **Why did the man refuse to go outside during a full moon?**

   He was afraid of moonstruck cows.

164. **How does the moon get his hair done?**

   Eclipse it.

165. **What's a vampire's favorite time of day?**

   Nighty-night.

166. **Why did the astronaut throw a party on the moon?**

   Because it had great space.

167. **What do you call an argument on the moon?**

   A lunar-tic attack.

168. **Why was the night sad?**

Because it didn't get any stars.

169. How do you organize a party in space?

You planet.

170. Why did the moon skip dinner?

It was full.

18. TRICK-OR-TREATING TRIUMPHS (TASTY TOTS FOR TOTS WHO ARE OUT TOTING)

171. Why did the skeleton go trick-or-treating?

To get some spare ribs.

172. What's a ghost's favorite candy?

Boo-ble gum.

173. Why did the kid dress up as a computer for Halloween?

To get some megabites.

174. What candy do vampires refuse to eat?

Lifesavers.

175. Why did the witch refuse to wear a flat hat?

There was no point.

176. What did the vampire say after trick-or-treating?

"Fangs for the memories!"

177. Why did the pirate bring a ladder trick-or-treating?

To reach the high seas (C's).

178. **How do monsters tell their fortunes on Halloween?**

With their horror-scopes.

179. **Why did the ghost refuse to trick-or-treat?**

He had no-body to go with.

180. **What's a mummy's favorite type of music while trick-or-treating?**

Wrap music.

19. COSTUME CATASTROPHES (CAT @$$ TROPHY)

181. **Why did the kid's vampire costume fail?**

He couldn't find his cape-abilities.

182. **What happened when the witch tried to fix her broken broom?**

She realized she couldn't handle it.

183. **Why did the ghost's costume look so cheap?**

He got it on a skeleton budget.

184. **What did Frankenstein say when he couldn't find a costume?**

"Guess I'll have to wing it!"

185. **Why did the zombie's costume fall apart?**

It was dead on arrival.

186. **How did the mummy feel when his costume unraveled?**

Totally wrapped up in the moment.

187. **Why was the werewolf's costume too tight?**

He didn't account for fur shrinkage.

188. **What did the pumpkin say when its costume didn't fit?**

"I guess I'm out of my gourd!"

189. **Why did the alien's costume get disqualified?**

It was too far out.

190. **What did the skeleton say when he couldn't find a costume?**

"I'm bone out of ideas!"

20. MAGICAL SPELL AND POTION PUNS (PUNISHMENT ENOUGH!)

191. **Why did the witch use GPS?**

She didn't want to spell lost.

192. **What do you call a potion that makes you disappear?**

Evapor-ate.

193. **Why was the wizard good at cooking?**

He knew how to stir up magic.

194. **How do witches stay positive?**

They use affirmations.

195. **What did the apprentice wizard say to his mentor?**

"You're the wand that I want!"

196. **Why did the witch fail her potion exam?**

She couldn't concentrate.

197. **What's a wizard's favorite dance move?**

The spell shuffle.

198. **Why did the wizard start recycling?**

He wanted to reduce, reuse, re-magic.

199. What do you call a magician on a plane?

A flying sorcerer.

200. How does a witch write in her diary?

In cursive.

A COLLECTION OF 200 SIDE-SPLITTING JOKES CATEGORIZED UNDER VARIOUS SPOOKY AND FUN-THEMED SECTIONS.

Get ready to laugh your way through Halloween, horror, and all things eerie!

1. HALLOWEEN HUMOR

1. **Why did the ghost go to school?**

   To learn how to be a better spook-tator!
2. **What do you get when you cross a vampire with a snowman?**

   Frostbite.
3. **Why don't mummies take vacations?**

   They're afraid they'll relax and unwind.
4. **What do you call a dancing ghost?**

   The Boogie-Man.
5. **Why did the scarecrow become a successful comedian?**

   Because he was outstanding in his field!
6. **What's a vampire's favorite fruit?**

   Neck-tarines.
7. **Why was the broom late for the Halloween party?**

   It over-swept!
8. **What kind of music do pumpkins listen to?**

   Gourd-geous tunes.
9. **Why did the skeleton go to the party alone?**

   He had no body to go with.

10. What do you call a witch who lives at the beach?

A sand-witch.

2. HORROR HILARITY

1. **Why are horror movies so cool?**

   They have killer plots!
2. **What do you call a dancing ghost in a horror movie?**

   The Boogie-Man.
3. **Why did the ghost apply for a job?**

   He needed some "spirit" in his resume.
4. **What's a horror movie villain's favorite exercise?**

   Deadlifts.
5. **Why don't ghosts like rain?**

   It dampens their spirits.
6. **How do horror characters stay in shape?**

   They run from their problems.
7. **What's a monster's favorite snack?**

   Munchies.
8. **Why did the zombie go to therapy?**

   He felt rotten inside.
9. **What do you call a horror movie about birds?**

   Flock-o'-lantern.
10. **Why was the vampire's computer always crashing?**

   He had too many bites.

3. SPOOKY STORIES SILLINESS

1. **Why did the ghost go to the party?**

   For the boos!

2. **What's a ghost's favorite dessert?**

   Ice scream.

3. **Why did the haunted house apply for a loan?**

   It needed a little spirit boost.

4. **What do you call a ghost who tells jokes?**

   A funny-bone.

5. **Why don't ghosts like elevators?**

   They're afraid of getting stuck between worlds.

6. **What's a ghost's favorite game?**

   Hide and shriek.

7. **Why did the ghost join the band?**

   He had great spirit.

8. **What do you call a ghost's true love?**

   His ghoul-friend.

9. **Why are ghosts bad liars?**

   Because you can see right through them.

10. **What kind of key does a ghost use to unlock his room?**

A spoo-key.

4. GOTHIC ROMANCE GIGGLES

1. **Why did the gothic couple go to the dance?**

   To have a hauntingly good time.
2. **What's a vampire's favorite romantic movie?**

   "Love at First Bite."
3. **Why did the ghost write a love letter?**

   To express his undying love.
4. **What do gothic romantics eat for dessert?**

   Black forest cake.
5. **Why did the vampire refuse to kiss during the day?**

   He didn't want to show his true colors.
6. **How do gothic lovers stay connected?**

   Through spirit messages.
7. **What's a werewolf's favorite romantic song?**

   "I'll Be Howling."
8. **Why did the gothic poet break up with his vampire girlfriend?**

   She was too draining.
9. **What do you call a romantic ghost story?**

   A love haunting.

10. **Why do gothic lovers never get lost?**

They always follow their heart's dark path.

---

5. CREEPY LEGENDS CHUCKLES

1. **Why don't legends ever get bored?**

   They always have a story to tell.
2. **What did the ghost say to the legendary hero?**

   "Boo to you too!"
3. **Why was the legend always calm?**

   Because it had a mythical mindset.
4. **What's a legendary creature's favorite game?**

   Hide and seek-er.
5. **Why did the unicorn refuse to join the legend?**

   It didn't want to be mythical.
6. **What do you call a legend who tells funny stories?**

   A myth-comedian.
7. **Why did the dragon apply for a job?**

   It wanted to breathe new life into its career.
8. **How do legends keep in touch?**

   Through fairy mail.
9. **What's a vampire's favorite legendary tale?**

   "Dracula's Laughter."
10. **Why do legends make terrible secret keepers?**

They always spill the myths.

6. FRIGHTENING FOLKLORE FUN

1. **Why did the folklore character become a comedian?**

   To scare up some laughs.
2. **What's a folklore monster's favorite dessert?**

   Rocky Road.
3. **Why don't folklore creatures use social media?**

   They prefer to keep it spooky.
4. **What do you call a folklore ghost who tells jokes?**

   A pun-derful spirit.
5. **Why was the folklore witch always happy?**

   She found her brew-tiful smile.
6. **How do folklore giants stay in shape?**

   They do lots of giant steps.
7. **What's a folklore creature's favorite season?**

   Spooktober.
8. **Why did the folklore troll start a band?**

   To bridge the gap between music and mischief.
9. **What's a folklore vampire's favorite accessory?**

   A blood-red tie.
10. **Why did the folklore banshee join a choir?**

She loved singing her wails.

7. MONSTER MADNESS

1. **Why did the monster go to school?**

   To improve his scare-ducation.
2. **What's a monster's favorite part of the day?**

   The fright of day.
3. **Why did the monster bring a suitcase to the comedy club?**

   He was ready to pack in the laughs.
4. **What do you call a friendly monster?**

   A good fiend.
5. **Why are monsters great at parties?**

   They bring all the boos.
6. **What's a monster's favorite sport?**

   Monster-boarding.
7. **Why did the monster join the gym?**

   To work on his roar-ing muscles.
8. **What do you call a monster with no neck?**

   A neck-less gorgon.
9. **Why did the monster go to therapy?**

   He had some deep-seated issues.
10. **What's a monster's favorite ice cream flavor?**

Chocolate scarie.

8. HAUNTED HOUSE HUMOR

1. **Why did the haunted house apply for a loan?**

   It needed a little spirit boost.
2. **What do you call a haunted house with great Wi-Fi?**

   A boo-tiful connection.
3. **Why was the haunted house always cold?**

   It had too many drafts.
4. **What's a haunted house's favorite type of music?**

   Rock and roll-ers.
5. **Why don't haunted houses ever get lost?**

   They always follow the ghostly GPS.
6. **What did the haunted house say to the new tenant?**

   "Welcome to your spooky abode!"
7. **Why was the haunted house a terrible liar?**

   It could never keep its doors closed.
8. **How do haunted houses stay in shape?**

   They do ghost squats.
9. **What's a haunted house's favorite drink?**

   Boos-brews.
10. **Why did the haunted house start a band?**

To raise some spirits.

9. GHOSTLY GIGGLES

1. **Why did the ghost go to the party?**

   To have a spook-tacular time.
2. **What's a ghost's favorite street?**

   A dead end.
3. **Why are ghosts bad at lying?**

   Because you can see right through them.
4. **What do ghosts wear when it rains?**

   Boo-ts.
5. **Why did the ghost go to the bar?**

   For the boos!
6. **How do ghosts send letters?**

   Through the ghost office.
7. **What's a ghost's favorite fruit?**

   Boo-berries.
8. **Why don't ghosts like parties?**

   They have no body to dance with.
9. **What's a ghost's favorite game?**

   Peek-a-boo.
10. **Why was the ghost a bad comedian?**

    His jokes were too transparent.

10. VAMPIRE VAUDEVILLE

1. Why did the vampire read the newspaper?

He heard it had great circulation.

2. What do vampires like to eat for breakfast?

A blood orange.

3. Why don't vampires have many friends?

Because they are a pain in the neck.

4. What's a vampire's favorite ice cream flavor?

Vein-illa.

5. How do vampires start a letter?

"Tomb it may concern..."

6. Why did the vampire go to art class?

He wanted to learn how to draw blood.

7. What do vampires use to brush their teeth?

Fang-tastic toothpaste.

8. Why are vampires like false teeth?

They come out at night.

9. What do you get when you cross a vampire with a snowman?

Frostbite.

10. Why did the vampire take a day off?

He was feeling a little drained.

11. WEREWOLF WIT

1. **Why did the werewolf go to the barber?**

   To get a fur-ocious cut.
2. **What's a werewolf's favorite music genre?**

   Howl-lywood pop.
3. **Why don't werewolves make good secret agents?**

   They always let the cat out of the bag.
4. **What do you call a werewolf who loves math?**

   A howl-gebrator.
5. **Why was the werewolf always tired?**

   He was dog-tired from all the howling.
6. **What's a werewolf's favorite dessert?**

   Moontastic marshmallows.
7. **Why did the werewolf apply for a job?**

   He wanted to earn his bones.
8. **How do werewolves keep their fur looking good?**

   With fur-estic hair products.
9. **Why did the werewolf join a gym?**

   To work on his howl-tones.
10. **What's a werewolf's favorite season?**

   Howl-oween.

12. ZOMBIE ZINGERS

1. **Why did the zombie go to school?**

   He wanted to improve his "dead"ucation.
2. **What's a zombie's favorite game?**

   Dead or Alive.
3. **Why don't zombies eat comedians?**

   They taste funny.
4. **What do you call a zombie who writes jokes?**

   A pun-ghoul.
5. **Why was the zombie a bad musician?**

   He had no rhythm in his dead beats.
6. **What's a zombie's favorite movie?**

   "Night of the Living Laughs."
7. **Why did the zombie bring a ladder to the party?**

   To reach the high spirits.
8. **How do zombies stay in shape?**

   They do dead-lifts.
9. **Why did the zombie go to therapy?**

   He felt he was going through a "dead" period.
10. **What do zombies wear to formal events?**

    Dead suits.

13. WITCHY WITTICISMS

1. **Why did the witch go to the doctor?**

   She felt broom-atose.
2. **What's a witch's favorite subject in school?**

   Spelling.
3. **Why don't witches like to ride their brooms when they're angry?**

   They're afraid of flying off the handle.
4. **What do witches use to do their hair?**

   Scare-spray.
5. **Why was the witch a great musician?**

   She had perfect broom-us.
6. **What's a witch's favorite ride at the amusement park?**

   The roller broom-ster.
7. **Why did the witch bring a ladder to the party?**

   To reach new heights in her spell-casting.
8. **What do you call a witch who lives at the beach?**

   A sand-witch.
9. **Why did the witch start a gardening business?**

   She had a green thumb for spells.

10. How do witches keep their hair in place?

With scare-spray.

---

14. SKELETON SNICKERS

1. **Why didn't the skeleton fight the zombie?**

   He didn't have the guts.
2. **What do skeletons say before they eat?**

   Bone appetit!
3. **Why are skeletons so calm?**

   Nothing gets under their skin.
4. **What's a skeleton's favorite musical instrument?**

   The trom-bone.
5. **Why did the skeleton go to the party alone?**

   He had no body to go with.
6. **How do skeletons call their friends?**

   On the tele-bone.
7. **What do you call a skeleton who won't work?**

   Lazy bones.
8. **Why did the skeleton stay home from the dance?**

   He had no body to dance with.
9. **What's a skeleton's favorite type of art?**

   Bone-etry.
10. **Why did the skeleton go to the barbecue?**

To get some spare ribs.

15. MUMMY MIRTH

1. **Why did the mummy go on a diet?**

   He wanted to keep his wraps slim.

2. **What did the mummy say when he was invited to dinner?**

   "That would be de-lightful!"

3. **Why was the mummy such a good listener?**

   He was all ears.

4. **What's a mummy's favorite kind of coffee?**

   De-coffin-ated.

5. **Why did the mummy open a bakery?**

   He was great at making wrap sandwiches.

6. **How do mummies keep their hair in place?**

   With scare-spray.

7. **Why was the mummy comedian so bad?**

   His jokes were ancient.

8. **What's a mummy's favorite flower?**

   Chrysanthemummies.

9. **Why did the mummy get promoted?**

   He was an up-and-comer.

10. **What's a mummy's favorite instrument?**

    The tomb-a.

16. PUMPKIN PUNS

1. **Why was the pumpkin late for the meeting?**

   It got stuck in a jam.
2. **What do you get when you drop a pumpkin?**

   Squash.
3. **How do you fix a broken pumpkin?**

   With a pumpkin patch.
4. **Why did the pumpkin turn red?**

   Because it saw the salad dressing.
5. **What did the pumpkin say to the carver?**

   "Cut it out!"
6. **Why do pumpkins sit on people's porches?**

   They have no hands to knock on the door.
7. **What did one Jack-o'-lantern say to the other on the way to the party?**

   "Let's get glowing!"
8. **What is a pumpkin's favorite sport?**

   Squash.
9. **Why did the pumpkin cross the road?**

   To get to the pumpkin patch.
10. **What did the scientist say to the pumpkin?**

    "You've got potential, let's carve out your future!"

17. BLACK CAT COMEDY

1. **Why do black cats never get lost?**

   They always find their way meow-t.
2. **What did the black cat say after a big meal?**

   "I'm feline fine!"
3. **Why did the black cat avoid mirrors?**

   He didn't want to risk bad luck.
4. **What do black cats like to eat on hot days?**

   Mice cream.
5. **Why are black cats good at video games?**

   They have nine lives.
6. **What's a black cat's favorite color?**

   Purr-ple.
7. **Why did the black cat sit on the mat?**

   To catch the morning mews.
8. **What did the superstitious person say when he saw a black cat?**

   "Guess I'm in fur a treat!"
9. **Why did the black cat start a band?**

   He had great mew-sical talent.

10. How do black cats celebrate Halloween?

They throw a cat-tastic party.

18. GRAVEYARD GUFFAWS

1. **Why did the zombie get lost in the graveyard?**

   He couldn't find his plot.
2. **What did one tombstone say to the other?**

   "I'm dying to tell you something!"
3. **Why are graveyards so noisy?**

   Because of all the coffin.
4. **How do ghosts like their steak?**

   Medium scare.
5. **What's a graveyard's favorite game?**

…(So very, very sorry…at this point…all the authors all perished…mysteriously…)

ILLUSTRATED AUTHOR BIOGRAPHIES

ILLUSTRATED AWE-THOR BIO"GRAFF"IES

Absolutely hilarious, funny, laugh-out-loud biographies for each of the authors of this joke book:

1. GHOSTS AND APPARITIONS

MISTY KNIGHT

Misty Knight isn't your average author—she's a spectral sleuth with a knack for uncovering the funniest apparitions and ghostly giggles. Born under a full moon in the foggy town of **Hauntsville**, Misty's early years were anything but ordinary. From a young age, she could see spirits attending her school assemblies and hear jokes from the other side, which sparked her lifelong passion for paranormal humor.

After graduating from the **Academy of Eerie Entertainment**, Misty decided to combine her two loves: writing and the supernatural. Armed with her trusty notebook and a flashlight (to keep the ghosts entertained during late-night writing sessions), she embarked on a mission to bring laughter to the haunted halls of literature. Her first book, **"Boo-Larious Tales: Laughs from the Other Side,"** became an instant bestseller among both the living and the dearly departed.

Misty's unique writing style blends spooky storytelling with side-splitting humor. Whether she's penning puns with poltergeists or crafting comedic capers with comical apparitions, Misty ensures that every page is filled with ghostly giggles. Her characters range from prankster phantoms who love to play hide-and-seek with the living to friendly spirits who can't help but chuckle at their own ethereal mishaps.

When she's not writing, Misty enjoys **haunting comedy clubs**, where she performs her own ghostly stand-up routines. Her signature act, **"Spectral Stand-Up,"** has audiences both human and supernatural roaring with laughter. Misty believes that laughter is the best way to bridge the gap between the living and the dead, proving that even in the afterlife, humor reigns supreme.

Misty Knight's latest project, **"Ghoul-ty by Association: A Hauntingly Funny Anthology,"** promises to be her most uproarious collection yet. Packed with tales of mischievous spirits, laugh-out-loud hauntings, and ghostly gags, this book is perfect for anyone who loves a good scare with a side of snickers.

In her downtime, Misty enjoys **ghost-hunting for jokes**, ensuring she never runs out of material to tickle her readers' funny bones. She also hosts a popular podcast, **"Laughs from the Beyond,"** where she interviews spirits about their funniest afterlife experiences.

Misty Knight invites you to join her on a hilariously haunted journey where every ghost has a giggle and every apparition brings a laugh. Whether you're a skeptic or a believer, her stories will have you laughing all the way to the graveyard and back. So grab a flashlight, keep an eye out for the mischievous mist, and prepare to be spookily amused by the one and only Misty Knight!

With Misty Knight's whimsical approach to the paranormal, her biography not only highlights her humorous take on ghosts and apparitions but also ensures readers are entertained from the very first page. Her blend of spooky charm and comedic flair makes her the perfect author for your laugh-out-loud Halloween joke book!

G. HOST

G. Host has been the life *after* the party since 1823. Despite being transparent about his intentions, he loves to keep readers in suspense - suspended animation technically. When he's not buried in his work he is busy haunting bestsellers lists, floating around literary circles - loves old libraries, making spirits bright.

PHANTOM WRITER

Phantom Writer penned his first invisible ink novel at the age of zero—because he doesn't exist! Often seen but never caught, he specializes in ghostwriting for the undead. Rumor has it he once scared the pants off a scarecrow with just a semicolon.

SPOOK E. SPECTER

Spook E. Specter, the eeriest pun-slinger in the afterlife, spends his days chilling in haunted mansions and his nights crafting jokes that will make you scream—with laughter. He's so good at what he does, it's scary!

2. VAMPIRES AND DRACULA

COUNT PEN-ULA

Count Pen-ula traded his cape for a quill long ago, sucking the ink out of pens instead of blood from necks. He's known for turning into a bat at the most inconvenient times—like during book signings. His fans find his work biting and irresistibly charming.

COUNT PUN-ULA

Count Pun-ula, the lesser-known yet undeniably punny cousin of Count Pen-ula, has been avoiding the limelight (and sunlight) for centuries. Hailing from the remote region of Transyl-laugh-nia, Count Punula has dedicated his eternal life to perfecting the art of the pun, much to the groans and delight of his captive audiences.

Unlike his bloodthirsty relatives, Count Pun-ula prefers to draw laughs rather than blood. He believes that the pen is mightier than the fang and has been known to literally charm the stakes off an angry mob with his witty one-liners. His favorite pastime is attending open mic nights at local taverns, where he slays the crowd without leaving a single bite mark.

Count Pun-ula's castle is said to be filled with echoes of laughter and the occasional bat who doubles as his comedy coach. When asked about his nocturnal lifestyle, he quips, "I'm just a night owl who's batty about puns!" He's also the founder of the Transylvanian Pun Preservation Society, aiming to keep the ancient art of wordplay undead and well.

He has a particular knack for turning grave situations into humorous anecdotes, and his coffin is rumored to double as a joke-writing desk. His memoir, *"From Dusk Till Pun: My Life in Bites,"* received *only* rave reviews (the other reviewers were later described as "batty" and never heard from again...!), with critics calling it "drop-dead hilarious" and "a real pain in the neck—in a good way!"

Count Pun-ula invites you to sink your teeth into his latest collection of side-splitting jokes. Just remember: laughter may not grant you eternal life, but with Count Punula, it sure makes the night fly by!

DR. ACULA

Dr. Acula, a retired hematologist, now focuses on writing sharp wit that doesn't require a prescription. He enjoys moonwalking moonlit walks, rare steaks, and avoiding wooden ones. His memoir *"Blood, Sweat, and Cheers"* topped the charts for centuries.

BELLA LUGIGGLES

Bella Lugiggles hails from Transyl-laugh-nia, where she cultivated her wicked sense of humor. She's been making audiences howl since she first stepped out of the shadows. When she's not cracking jokes, she's practicing her sinister laugh—it's to die for!

3. ZOMBIES AND THE UNDEAD

RAY N. CARNATION

Ray N. Carnation

Ray N. Carnation

Ray N. Carnation has been making audiences laugh through countless lifetimes, proving that good humor truly transcends existence. Reincarnated as a perennial punster, Ray has mastered the art of eternal comedy, bringing fresh laughs with each new incarnation.

Born in the mystical realm of **Eternal Evergreen**, Ray's first life was as a mischievous garden gnome, where he honed his skills in stealthy puns and root-in-the-ground humor. After several lifetimes as a witty woodland sprite and a giggling garden fairy, Ray discovered his true calling: spreading laughter across every reincarnation.

"WHAT IN TARNATION??!?" - ROY N. CARNATION - RAY'S FATHER UPON FINDING RAY REINCARNATED - THE FIRST TIME.

In his latest life as **Ray N. Carnation**, he seamlessly blends his ancient comedic wisdom with modern-day humor. Whether he's performing in haunted forests, spooky gardens, or mystical meadows, Ray's jokes are always in full bloom— though he prefers to keep flower humor to a minimum. One of his favorites: "Why did the scarecrow become a successful comedian? Because he was outstanding in his field!"

Ray's unique perspective on life and laughter allows him to connect with audiences on a soul-deep level. His timeless routines often explore the hilarious side of reincarnation, like accidentally remembering past lives and mixing up his punchlines from previous existences. Audiences can't help but chuckle as Ray navigates the complexities of eternal life with a twinkle in his eye and a joke on his lips.

When he's not performing, Ray enjoys meditating on the mysteries of existence and perfecting his reincarnation-related humor. His bestselling book, *"Laughing Through the Ages: A Reincarnated Comedian's Guide to Eternal Giggles,"* offers timeless tips on keeping your humor fresh across lifetimes.

Ray N. Carnation invites you to join him on a never-ending journey of laughter, where every joke is a rebirth of hilarity and every punchline is a fresh start. Embrace the cycle of comedy and let Ray's reincarnated wit keep you laughing for eternity!

SUNTA B.A. GHOUL

Sunta B.A. Ghoul is the reigning queen of zombie humor and the undead chuckle champion of the literary world. Hailing from the eerie yet enchanting town of **Graveyard Grove**, Sunta discovered her passion for the macabre and the hilarious at an early age—quite literally. Legend has it that she was first bitten by a zombie during a school play, which not only gave her eternal life but also an everlasting appetite for puns and punchlines.

After graduating with honors from **Necro-Nonsense University**, where she double-majored in **Zombietology** and **Ghoul-ology**, Sunta embarked on a mission to prove that even the most flesh-craving creatures have a funny bone. Her debut collection, **"Braaains and Banter: Laughs from the Undead,"** quickly became a staple at both living and dead gatherings, proving that humor truly transcends life and death.

Sunta's unique comedic style blends the spine-tingling suspense of zombie lore with side-splitting satire. Whether she's penning tales of the **Gratefully Dead** band that never took a break or crafting jokes about zombies who can't quite get their act together, Sunta ensures that every page is filled with laughs that are to die for. One of her favorite jokes: **"Why don't zombies eat comedians? They taste funny!"**

When she's not writing, Sunta enjoys hosting **"Rotten Routines,"** a popular podcast where she interviews fellow undead comedians about their funniest afterlife experiences. Her live performances are legendary, featuring a mix of stand-up routines, zombie impressions, and interactive segments where audience members can "join the horde"—figuratively, of course.

Sunta's latest masterpiece,

"The Gratefully Dead and Other Hilarious Horrors,"

is a rip-roaring collection that delves into the lighter side of undead existence. From stories of zombies trying to maintain a social life to ghouls grappling with modern technology, Sunta tackles it all with a humorous twist that leaves readers both terrified and tickled.

In her downtime, Sunta enjoys **brain-freezing ice cream socials** (because even zombies need a sweet treat), **moonlit comedy improv**, and **haunted house karaoke**, where she belts out hits like "Thriller" and "Zombie Shuffle" with impeccable undead enthusiasm. She's also an avid collector of **punny tombstones**, each engraved with her favorite one-liners, ensuring that even in the afterlife, laughter never dies. Watch for her book coming out!:

Punny Tombstones: Even the Dead Have Sense...of Humor!! - A "working title"

Sunta B.A. Ghoul believes that laughter is the best medicine— even if you're a zombie with a taste for brains. Her infectious humor and love for all things undead make her the perfect author for *"Laugh-Out-Loud Halloween: 666 Spooktacular Jokes & Author Biographies"* Whether you're a living lover of laughter or an undead aficionado of amusement, Sunta guarantees that her jokes will keep you coming back for more, no matter how many lifetimes it takes.

Join Sunta B.A. Ghoul on her hilariously haunted journey through the world of zombies and the undead, where every joke is a bite-sized laugh and every story is a rotting good time. Embrace the fun side of the frightful and let Sunta's humor resurrect your spirits this Halloween season!

With **Sunta B.A. Ghoul** at the helm, your joke book is sure to be a delightful blend of spooky and silly, perfect for readers who love their Halloween with a hearty side of humor!

ANITA REST

Anita Rest was once a hardworking corporate lawyer until she decided to "live a little"—ironically, after becoming undead. Now, she spends her time advocating for zombie rights and napping during the daylight hours - resting in peace. Her motto: "Why hustle when you can shuffle?"

MORT TISHEN

Mort Tishen has been decomposing music and jokes since he stopped pushing up *daisies* and *rose* to fame—or rather, rose from the grave. He has taken no time off since he was offed. Always picks up the check ever since he checked out. He believes in equal opportunity for all zombies to enjoy brains and puns alike. His humor is grave, but his timing is killer.

ZED DEADMAN

Zed Deadman, voted both "Most likely to go on tour following the Dead around" and "Most Likely to Eat Your Brains" in high school, stumbled into comedy after tripping over his own feet. He's a no-brainer when it comes to making audiences laugh, though sometimes his jokes fall apart—literally.

4. WITCHES AND WIZARDS

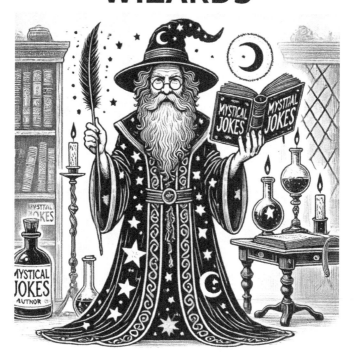

WANDA WITCHFUL THINKING

Wanda hails from the whimsical woods of Enchantington, where the cauldrons are always bubbling, and the jokes are always brewing. Born into a long line of spell-binding comedians, Wanda inherited not just her family's magical powers but also their wicked sense of humor.

From a young age, Wanda showed a knack for turning mishaps into laughter—like the time she accidentally turned her entire class into frogs and then taught them to sing in harmony. Realizing that her true magic lay in making people laugh, she enrolled in the prestigious Gigglewarts School of Witchcraft and Wizardry.

At Gigglewarts, Wanda majored in Pun-craft and minored in Chuckle Charms. Her thesis, "The Hilarious Effects of Tickling Spells on Trolls," received top honors and a few grunts of approval from the trolls themselves. She graduated magna cum cackle and was voted "Most Likely to Bewitch an Audience."

Wanda's stand-up career took off after her debut show, "Witchful Thinking," where she had the crowd levitating with laughter. She's known for her signature spell "Riddikulous-laughus," which transforms fears into hysterics. When asked about her comedic inspirations, she cites the Three Wiz-keteers and Merlin Monroe.

In her spare time, Wanda enjoys brewing up new jokes in her pun-derground lair and flying her broomstick in stand-up comedy clubs around the world. She insists that her broomstick has a mind of its own, often taking detours to comedy festivals and open mic nights.

Despite her magical prowess, Wanda remains humble. "After all," she says, "I'm just a witch trying to scratch that laugh itch." She's on a mission to prove that laughter is the best potion, and so far, audiences agree—her shows are spell-tacular!

Wanda Witchful Thinking invites you to join her on a magical journey where the laughs are enchanting and the punchlines come with a dash of pixie dust. Just be careful—you might leave her show with your sides split and your face transfigured into a permanent smile!Wanda Spell

Wanda Spell graduated top of her class from Broomstick Academy, majoring in Puns and Potions. When she's not brewing up laughs, she's turning princes into frogs—because everyone could use a good ribbit. Her spellbinding performances leave audiences enchanted.

ALBUS PUNBLEDORE

Albus Punbledore, headmaster of Wit-ards School of Laughcraft and Pun-ery, has been casting laughter spells for decades. His beard may be long, but his jokes are short and snappy. He's the chosen one when it comes to magical humor.

WIZARD OF AHHS

The Wizard of Ahhs has been behind the curtain of comedy for years, pulling laughter out of his hat. He journeyed down the punchline road to bring humor to all. His fans say there's no place like his shows for a good laugh.

5. WEREWOLVES AND SHAPE-SHIFTERS

LEIF N. SHIVERS

Leif N. Shivers prowls the comedy scene with the stealth and charm of a full moonlit night. Born under the eerie glow of a wolf's howl in the mystical village of **Lunaris Grove**, Leif discovered his passion for humor when he accidentally turned his pet dog into a comedian—a mishap that left both of them howling with laughter.

From a young age, Leif was fascinated by the mysterious world of werewolves and shapeshifters. While other kids played with action figures, he crafted pun-tastic tales of moonlit misadventures and fur-filled follies. His talent for blending spooky folklore with side-splitting humor earned him the nickname **"The Howling Humorist"** among his peers.

After graduating from **Moonshadow University** with a degree in **Cryptic Comedy and Shapeshifter Studies**, Leif embarked on a mission to prove that even the most fearsome creatures have a funny bone. His debut stand-up special, **"Fur Real Funny,"** had audiences roaring with laughter—or shivering from the sheer pun-derfulness of his jokes. Whether he's transforming into his werewolf persona on stage or shifting shapes to deliver the perfect punchline, Leif ensures that every performance is an unforgettable howl of hilarity.

Leif's unique comedic style effortlessly navigates the fine line between laughter and spine-tingling shivers. His jokes about shapeshifters often leave audiences in stitches, while his werewolf humor can send chills down even the bravest spines. One of his favorites: **"Why did the werewolf apply for a job at the bakery? Because he kneaded the dough!"** It's this perfect blend of clever wordplay and spooky charm that makes Leif N. Shivers a standout in the realm of horror comedy.

When he's not performing, Leif enjoys **moonlit improv sessions** with fellow supernatural beings, where he experiments with new puns and transforms everyday scenarios into howling good laughs. He's also the proud author of *"Shifting Gears: A Werewolf's Guide to Comedy,"* a bestseller that explores the humorous side of transformation and the challenges of maintaining a double life—both furry and funny.

Leif N. Shivers's latest project, **"Paws and Reflect: Laughs from the Lycanthropic Lens,"** promises to be his most chillingly comedic collection yet. Packed with tales of mischievous moonlight escapades, shapeshifter shenanigans, and werewolf witticisms, this book is perfect for anyone who loves a good scare with a side of snickers.

In his downtime, Leif enjoys **howling at the moon, chasing his own shadow for the perfect joke**, and **hosting late-night comedy marathons** that leave audiences either laughing uncontrollably or shivering from the delightful dread of his puns. He firmly believes that humor is the best way to bridge the gap between the living and the supernatural, proving that even in the darkest nights, laughter can light the way.

Join Leif N. Shivers on his transformative journey through comedy, where every joke is a shift in perspective and every punchline packs a bite. Whether you're a fan of werewolves, shapeshifters, or just love a good laugh under the moonlight, Leif guarantees that his humor will leave you howling with joy or shivering with amusement. Embrace the chill and chuckle along with **Leif N. Shivers**, the punniest predator in the comedy wilderness!

With **Leif N. Shivers** at the helm of werewolf and shapeshifter humor, his biography captures the essence of a comedian who masterfully intertwines spooky themes with pun-tastic brilliance. His ability to leave audiences either laughing or shivering:

> *"Wow! That was truly horrific!"* - *(Author diseased then... deceased)*

from his cleverly bad puns makes him the perfect addition to your laugh-out-loud Halloween joke book!

WARREN WOLFE

Warren Wolfe is a part-time comedian, full-time lycanthrope who howls at his own jokes—even when no one else does. He claims his humor is best appreciated during the full moon, and his stand-up routines are always a howling success.

LYCAN B. NORMAL

Lycan B. Normal insists he's just your average guy—except once a month when he becomes a pun-thirsty werewolf. He enjoys long walks in the moonlight and chasing cars (literally). His comedy is transformative!

FURREST HOWLINGTON

Furrest Howlington comes from a long line of distinguished werewolves. He writes his jokes on flea collars and delivers them with a bark and a bite. Offstage, he advocates for better representation of werewolves in horror comedies.

6. MONSTERS AND CREATURES

FRANK N. STEIN

Dave Jordano

Frank N. Stein last spotted here in this rare photo of him (see if you can spot him) at his day job: selling hot dogs and beer (the cruel owner thought the play on his name was hilarious - apparently why Frank ripped this building down - luckily it was before any customers had arrived - and ran off eating and drinking - burping and frankfurtering - and dragging the entire building and the poor, utterly fumigated, "outgassed" staff behind him - never to be seen again!)

Frank was stitched together ("A stitch in time saves nine!" his eponymous father, the good doctor, would always say!) from the funniest parts of other comedians. He assures us that any resemblance to other monsters is purely coincidental.

Since his horror filled B&E incident...

Building Ending, as some called it, or, others called it:

Blowing-his-big -brown-butt-bugle and

Extremely-explosive- exterminating-eggination

- of the entire town/county - as it came to be known...some say he could bake brownies with his backdoor breeze and that his behind belching broke the sound barrier without a plane...and, sadly, some of the staff did not make it...home til morning, anyway...

Since then, he's electrified audiences worldwide and, though, sometimes *he* falls to pieces on stage, he always brings the building down...in laughter!

BEASTLY WRITERSON

Beastly Writerson, known for his monstrous appetite for humor, writes jokes that are larger than life. When he's not penning comical creatures, he's auditioning for roles under beds and in closets. He believes every day is Halloween if you try hard enough.

MON STARR

Mon Starr fell to Earth with a mission: to make humans laugh before the invasion. His otherworldly sense of humor has been called "out of this world." He's a star in every galaxy, but he still insists he's just a humble monster next door.

7. HAUNTED HOUSES

MANOR O. FEAR

THE MANOR O. FEAR

Manor O. Fear inherited his haunted estate from a long line of ghouls and goblins. He invites you to stay awhile—perhaps an eternity—and enjoy his hospitality and ghostly humor. His jokes always bring the house down.

HAUNT E. MANSION

Haunt E. Mansion is more than just a pretty façade. She's the leading lady of haunted real estate comedy. With doors that creak on cue and walls that have ears (literally), she ensures that laughter echoes through every corridor.

JOHNNY N. SHINING

Johnny N. Shining spends his time roaming empty hallways and writing jokes that will make you question your sanity. He's a master at turning everyday hotel experiences into paranormal punchlines. Just don't ask about Room 237.

8. SKELETONS AND BONES

DUSTIN BONES

Dustin Bones has always had a knack for digging up the funniest jokes—literally! Born in the marrow of a bustling comedy club, Dustin's early life was filled with laughter echoing through hollow halls. As a skeleton with a spine for humor, he decided early on that life without flesh was no excuse to skip leg day... or punchlines.

After graduating **Boneyard University** with a degree in **Humorous Osteology**, Dustin embarked on a quest to prove that even the bare bones of a joke can tickle the funny bone of any audience. His debut stand-up special, **"Rib-Tickling Ribs,"** had audiences rolling in the aisles—or should we say, rolling over their chairs in laughter.

When he's not busy rattling with laughter, Dustin enjoys **bone-appétit cooking classes**, where he whips up side-splitting recipes like **"Funny Bone Broth"** and **"Humerus Hamburgers."** He's also an avid collector of **pun-derwear**, ensuring he's always prepared to crack a joke or two at a moment's notice.

Dustin's unique ability to keep things light-hearted, even when dealing with his skeletal frame, has earned him the title of **"The Bone-afide Comedian."** His books, including the bestseller *"Bone Jokes That'll Make You Rattle"*, are a testament to his enduring legacy in the world of spooky humor.

Whether he's performing at haunted houses, graveyards, or just hanging out with his fellow bone buddies, Dustin Bones proves that laughter truly is the best medicine—even if you're all bones!

SKEL E. TON

Skel E. Ton may be all bones, but he's got a lot of heart—somewhere. He rattles audiences with his bone-dry wit and never shies away from a bare-bones joke. When asked how he keeps so fit, he says, "No guts, no glory!"

ANITA BODY

Anita Body has been searching for her missing pieces ever since she fell apart laughing at one of her own jokes. She believes in living life to the fullest—even if she's just a skeleton of her former self. Her humor is rib-ticklingly good.

CAL C. UM

Cal C. Um is the backbone of any comedy show he joins. He keeps his audience's spirits high with his humerus one-liners. Though he lacks flesh, his jokes have plenty of meat on them.

9. MUMMIES AND ANCIENT CURSES

PHARAOH MOANS

Pharaoh Moans has been unwrapping laughter for over 3,000 years. He's known for his deadpan delivery and timeless jokes. When he's not entertaining, he's just chilling in his tomb, taking life one wrap at a time.

WRAPSODY JONES

Wrapsody Jones is the queen of the undead scene, weaving tales that leave audiences in stitches. She's a classic triple threat: she can walk, groan, and deliver punchlines—all while bound in linen. Her performances are a wrap!

ANNIE TUT

Annie Tut, distant cousin of King Tut, brings a feminine touch to the mummy comedy circuit. She believes that laughter is the best medicine—unless you're cursed, then maybe try an amulet. She guarantees her jokes are old but gold.

10. PUMPKINS AND JACK-O'-LANTERNS

JACK O. LANTERN

Jack O. Lantern lights up the room wherever he goes. With a face that's always beaming, he's carved out a niche in the comedy world. He spends his off-season teaching others how to glow with confidence.

GORD N. ORANGE

Gord N. Orange is the self-proclaimed "King of the Patch." He squashes the competition with his seedy humor. Though he's often hollow inside, his jokes are filled to the brim with pulp and wit.

AUTUMN CARVER

Autumn Carver wields her pen like a sharp knife, cutting right to the funny bone. She specializes in seasonal humor and believes that life is gourd-geous when you're laughing. She's a slice above the rest

11. BLACK CATS AND SUPERSTITIONS

FELIX OMEN

Felix Omen crossed your path to bring you good luck and great laughs. Despite the rumors, he insists he's not bad luck—unless you're allergic to hilarity. He spends his free time knocking over punchlines and napping in sunbeams.

KITTY K. LURE

Kitty K. Lure has captivated audiences with her purr-fect timing and claws-out humor. She believes every life should be filled with laughter—all nine of them. She's not kitten around when it comes to comedy.

WHISKERS MC LUCK

Whiskers McLuck considers himself the luckiest cat alive, especially after dodging that falling piano. He brings a feline finesse to his jokes, leaving audiences feline good. His motto: "Stay curious and keep them laughing."

12. GRAVEYARDS
AND TOMBSTONES

PHIL GRAVES

Phil Graves has been digging up laughs since the dawn of time. As a graveyard shift worker, he moonlights as a comedian who knows how to bury a joke and resurrect it later. He assures fans his humor is anything but dead.

DOUG M. DEEP

Doug M. Deep is in too deep with his graveyard humor, but he wouldn't have it any other way. He specializes in dark comedy that's six feet under but always goes over well. His career is proof that you can dig yourself out of any hole.

HUGHES MORT STONE

"Use more stone!!" Hughes Mort Stone is as solid as a rock when it comes to delivering tombstone humor. He carves his jokes with precision, leaving no epitaph unturned. His fans say his performances are monumental. Watch for his pun filled tombstone comedy book by PERFECT PUBLISHING!

13. SPOOKY SOUNDS AND NOISES

ECHO HOWL

Echo Howl has made a sound decision to pursue a career in comedy...comedy...comedy... Reverberating through the halls of humor, she ensures her jokes are always heard twice...twice...! When not performing, she enjoys yodeling into canyons and scaring campers....campers...campers...campers...scamper...scamper... scamper away campers...before it's...too late...too late...too late...too late...

WHIS PER WIND

Whis Per Wind is a breath of fresh air in the comedy scene. Her soft-spoken jokes rustle through audiences like leaves on a quiet night. She believes the key to great humor is to leave them whispering for more.

CREE KEY DOOR

Cree Key Door opens up a world of laughter with every performance. His jokes may be a little squeaky, but they always swing back into style. He's known for keeping audiences on the edge—of their seats.

14. FULL MOONS
AND NIGHTTIME

LUNA TICK

Luna Tick is crazy about comedy and the moon. By day, she's nowhere to be found, but by night, she brings lunacy to new heights. She's sure to get under your skin...and stay there. Her humor is out of this world, and her timing is, well, once in a blue moon. Watch the clock and don't fall asleep under the full moon or you just might...join her...tick...tick...tick...tick...

STELLA KNIGHT

Stella Knight, Misty Knight's cousin and Batty Knight's niece, shines brightest when the sun goes down. Guiding audiences through the galaxy of giggles, she sprinkles stardust on every joke. She's proof that humor is the best way to reach for the stars.

N. SOMNIA

N. Somnia hails from Seattle (wink!) and hasn't slept - a wink - since 1923, and it shows—in his hilarious, sleep-deprived humor. His insomnia might be a curse, but it's a dream come true for comedy fans. He promises his creepy, hauntin jokes will keep you up at night.

15. TRICK-OR-TREATING ADVENTURES

CANDY CORNWELL

Candy Cornwell has a sweet tooth for humor. She goes door to door collecting laughs and handing out sugary puns. She believes life is like a bag of candy—you never know which joke you're gonna get.

TREAT A. LOT

Treat A. Lot is nobility in the kingdom of confections. Batty Knight is his Sir Pants-a-lot. He quests for the Holy Grail of giggles and believes that every joke is a treasure to be shared. His motto: "Trick me once, treat me twice!"

DORA BELLE

Dora Belle rings in the fun with her charming knock-knock jokes. She's always opening new doors in comedy and never leaves a welcome mat unturned. Audiences can't help but answer when she comes calling. Watch for her latest Knock Knock jokes book to come calling...soon!!

16. COSTUME MISHAPS

WARD ROBE
MALFUNCTION

(So sorry but we cannot afford to show you any of Mr. Function...ever...way, way too risky business) Ward Robe Malfunction has made a career out of fashion faux pas and comedic catastrophes. He believes the best way to dress for success is to embrace your mistakes—literally. His shows are a wardrobe whirlwind you won't want to miss.

ZOWIE BUTTON

Zowie Button stitches together humor with threads of absurdity. She patches up bad days with laughter and hems in the audience with her needle-sharp wit. She warns: "If you see me with a seam ripper, run!"

ZIP PEAR GONE

ZIP PEAR GONE

Zip Peaar a: author who always always flies by the seat of his pants.

Zip Pear Gone is always flying by the seat of his pants—especially when the zipper's broken. His comedy is held together by safety pins and a prayer. He zips through his setlist - because his clothing is failing and, well, he nevers knows when the end is coming - but he always leaves audiences....in stitches.

17. MAGIC SPELLS
AND POTIONS

AL K. MIST

Al K. Mist appears out of thin air to amaze and amuse. He's disappeared more rabbits than he can count and sawed more women in half than he cares to admit. His jokes are magical mishaps that always enchant.

POTION IVY

Potion Ivy brews jokes that are both toxic and intoxicating. She plants seeds of laughter wherever she goes, though some find her humor a bit viney. She always makes everyone scratch their itch...for comedy! She assures her fans that her act grows on you —eventually.

BREWSTER SPELLMAN

Brewster Spellman stirs up laughs with his cauldron of comedy. He mixes eye of newt with a dash of sarcasm to create potions that bubble over with humor. Just beware of the occasional explosive punchline.

18. SCARECROWS AND CORNFIELDS

CORNELIUS CROW

Cornelius Crow stands tall in the field of corny comedy. He's outstanding in his area and knows how to keep the birds and the audience away—or at least in stitches. His humor is corny, but that's the point: moans and groans!! Way more fun!!

HAYDEN FIELDS

Hayden Fields may seem a bit stiff, but he's got a heart of straw. He sows seeds of laughter and reaps hearty applause. Offstage, he enjoys just hanging around and watching the grass grow.

SCARY CROWLEY

Scary Crowley caws his way into the hearts of comedy fans everywhere. He believes that laughter is the best scare. His performances are the *stuff* of legend—or at least, the *stuff* that keeps crows up at night.

19. BATS AND NOCTURNAL CREATURES

BATTY DAY VIS

Batty Day Vis swoops into the literary scene with the grace of a bat at midnight and the wit of a seasoned Golden Girl —specifically, a charmingly cheeky Sophia. While she bears a striking resemblance to Sophia Petrillo from *The Golden Girls*, (all rumored to be...undead!) complete with a penchant for sharp one-liners and a timeless sense of humor, Batty Day Vis has no living relationship or undead ties—her jokes are as unique and lively as her fluttering wings.

Born under the shimmering glow of a full moon in the mysterious town of **Nocturna Hollow**, Batty developed an early, "nutty" fascination with bats and all things nocturnal. Her childhood was filled with evenings spent whispering secrets to the winged creatures and nights crafting puns that only the owls and moths could appreciate. Determined to share her lunar love for these misunderstood night dwellers, Batty pursued a degree in **Cryptozoological Comedy** from the prestigious **Shadowlight University**.

Batty's breakthrough came with her debut book, **"Wing It! Hilarious Tales from the Twilight Zone,"** where she masterfully blends spooky folklore with side-splitting humor. Her unique storytelling style, reminiscent of Sophia's wisecracks, brings bats and nocturnal creatures to life with a comedic twist that leaves readers hooting with laughter.

Known for her signature phrase, **"Let's batten down the laughs!"**, Batty Day Vis hosts the wildly popular podcast **"Night Flight Funnies,"** where she interviews nocturnal creatures about their funniest midnight mishaps and shares her own bat-inspired puns. Her live performances are legendary, with audiences captivated by her ability to turn the darkest nights into uproarious evenings filled with guffaws and giggles.

When she's not writing or performing, Batty enjoys **moonlit comedy improv**, where she often teams up with actual bats for spontaneous, wing-flapping punchlines. Her favorite hobby? **Bat yoga**, where she stretches her comedic muscles alongside her bat friends, ensuring she stays flexible enough to tackle any joke that comes her way.

Batty Day Vis's latest masterpiece, **"Echoes of Laughter: Tales from the Dark,"** promises to be her most enchanting collection yet. Packed with stories of mischievous bats, wise old owls, and the occasional giggling ghost (a nod to her Sophia-esque inspiration), this book is perfect for anyone who loves a good scare with a side of snickers.

In a world where night often brings fear, Batty Day Vis lights up the darkness with her radiant humor and infectious laughter. She believes that even the most shadowy corners can be illuminated with a good joke, proving that laughter truly is the best nightlight.

Join Batty Day Vis on her nocturnal journey through comedy, where every bat has a joke, every owl has a punchline, and every night is filled with laughter. Whether you're a night owl, a day dweller, or just someone who loves a good laugh under the stars, Batty Day Vis guarantees you'll leave her shows and books with wings of joy and hearts full of delight.

With Batty Day Vis's vibrant personality and her knack for turning the spooky into the silly, her biography perfectly captures the essence of a bat-loving, night-humored comedian who brings the spirit of *The Golden Girls* into the realm of nocturnal hilarity. Her blend of ghostly charm and batty humor makes her the perfect author for your laugh-out-loud Halloween joke book!

BATTY KNIGHT

Batty Knight swoops into the comedy scene with echolocation precision. He spends his nights hanging out in "caves" and his days avoiding the flash of the paparazzi - or anything giving any light...his tiny fury head constantly pounding from every utterly insane nocturnal mis-adventure. That's how he earned his moniker: one horrificiallly nightmarishly bad late night decision after the other. Always doing the right thing...batly!. From his birth to...today. His jokes are so good, they're worth staying up all night for.

OWL F.T.R. HOURS

Owl F.T.R. Hours gives a hoot about comedy.

He's wise beyond his years,

stays up well beyond his peers,

and stays sharp by keeping one eye open...

...on your fears.

He asks audiences, "Who's ready to laugh?" and they always respond,

"Who isn't?"

"Who's not?"

"Who else?"

"Who ain't"

"Who is?"

"Who's there?"

(Another plug for yet another **Perfect Publishing** publication:

"No, No, No...More Knock, Knock Jokes")

...

"Who???"

BEN N. DARKNESS

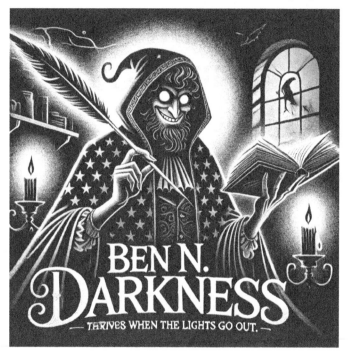

Ben N. Darkness thrives when the lights go out. He's a creature of habit—and that habit is making people laugh. He assures fans that while his humor may be dark (very, very, very dark) it's always illuminating.

20. ALIEN ENCOUNTERS AND UFOS

AL E. N.

Al E. N. comes in peace—and with a two-drink minimum. He's been orbiting the comedy clubs, abducting audiences with his otherworldly humor. He figures if Earthlings won't laugh, there are plenty of other planets to try.

MARTIAN WELLS

Martian Wells has been broadcasting laughs across the cosmos. He warns us that the invasion has already begun—and it's hilarious. His stories are so good, they're practically out of this world.

U.F. OWEN

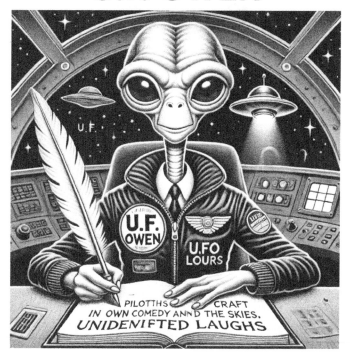

U.F. Owen has been unidentified for years, and he likes it that way. He pilots his own craft—both in comedy and in the skies. His jokes have been known to cause unexplained bursts of laughter. "Keep on U.F.O.-in'!!"

END-OF-BOOK REVIEW PAGE

There is still more book to read after this brief request...so please, everything...afterwards...

KEEP THE LAUGHTER HAUNTING!

Subtitle: Spread The Fun Like It's A Full Moon Party!

Well, well, well, look who's finished reading

"Laugh-Out-Loud Hilarious Halloween & Horror Humor: 666 Spook-tacularly Funny Jokes & Spooky Silly Stories of Authors' Biographies!"

You must be a true joke master now. You've laughed, you've groaned, your family and friends have moaned - and you might've even howled like a werewolf at midnight!

But now it's time to pass the torch (or should I say, the jack-o'-lantern?) and share this laughter with others. How? By leaving a review on Amazon!

Your review will help other readers discover this collection of ghostly giggles and spine-tingling silliness. And you'll be helping keep the spirit of Halloween humor alive!

So, if you had a blast reading these jokes, sharing a laugh, and maybe even learning some spooky author trivia, I'd be eternally (get it?!) grateful if you'd share your thoughts with the world.

Aim any smartphone camera at the
Black and White Q R Code above and
click OK to go to the link to review:
Laugh-Out-Loud Hilrious Halloween
& Horror Humor

Or please, try copying or clicking on the link below:

https://www.amazon.com/review/review-your-purchases/?
asin=B0DJ9NB2NG

**OR: Please, go to   www.Amazon.com   and search for this
title in order to leave a review. We cannot possibly thank you
enough!!**

Thank you for being part of this hilariously haunted journey,
and for helping us keep the game of laughter and spooky humor
alive!

Your Joke Ghost-writers,

*Varius N. Sundry - with Miss A. Laneous & the Rest of the Team
(RIP!!)*

ABOUT THE AUTHOR

Miss A. Laneous

Miss A. Laneous
B. 4/23/13 D. 10/31/78

The co-author of "LOL Hilarious Halloween & Horror Humor", is a whirlwind of weirdness and wit, a woman of a thousand oddities—and at least half of them are mismatched socks.

Known for her knack for turning even the most mundane of moments into comedic chaos, Miss Laneous' brain is a spooky-fun house, where ghouls slip on banana peels and vampires try to navigate online dating.

Rumor has it, she once scared off a poltergeist with a knock-knock joke and accidentally summoned a demon while ordering pizza.

With her wild ideas and knack for spooky silliness, she's the perfect partner for Varius N. Sundry, making sure horror has never been funnier... or more utterly absurd!

ABOUT THE AUTHOR

Varius N. Sundry

Varius N. Sundry
B. 3/13/13 D. 10/31/84

The mysterious ringleader of "LOL Hilarious Halloween & Horror Humor", is a master of the bizarre and the absurd, with a name as strange as the stories he curates.

Legend has it, Sundry was born under a blood moon in a haunted library, raised on a diet of bad puns and cursed manuscripts.

He has an uncanny ability to gather the most eccentric writers, luring them in with promises of bottomless candy corn and eternal giggles.

With a mind sharper than a vampire's tooth and a sense of humor darker than a witch's cauldron, Sundry stitches together tales that make you laugh till your spine tingles.

A true maestro of mirthful mayhem, he's the mastermind behind the creepiest comedy anthology to ever make you shriek and snicker at the same time.

NOW KEEP RIGHT
ON READING TO
CHECK OUT ALL THE
OTHER AMAZINGLY
AWESOME BOOKS BY
OUR PUBLISHER:

PERFECT PUBLISHING!

PERFECT PUBLISHING-BOOKS IN THIS SERIES: SCI-FI, HORROR, POP CULTURE - NOVELS, SHORT STORIES, TRIVIA AND JOKE BOOKS

Laugh-Out-Loud Hilarious Halloween & Horror Humor-666 Spook-Tacularly Funny Jokes & Scary Silly Stories Of Author Bios: Haunting Ghostly Giggling Guffaws, Creepy Corny Cackles, Witty Witchy Wickedness

Why did the undead chicken cross the road?
To get to end the fool.

Knock, knock!!
Who's there?
...
The undead chicken

Unknown undead

Get Ready to Howl with Laughter This Halloween!

Are you prepared for a spine-tingling, side-splitting adventure?
Dive into

Laugh-Out-Loud Hilarious Halloween & Horror Humor: 666 Spook-tacularly Hilarious Jokes & Funny Scary Author Biography Stories,

the ultimate collection of hilarious Halloween humor that will tickle your funny bone & leave you cackling like a witch!

A Haunting Collection for All Ages

666 Hilarious Jokes & Stories: Explore 20 eerie categories, from Ghosts & Apparitions to Alien Encounters & UFOs.

Family-Friendly Fun: Clean humor that's perfect for kids, teens, & adults alike.

Perfect for Any Occasion: Ideal for Halloween/Horror parties, sleepovers, classroom activities, or a fun night in.

Available in All Formats

Kindle eBook: Instant access to laughter on any device.

Paperback & Hardcover: A great addition to your coffee table or bookshelf.

Kindle Audiobook: Let the spooky tales come to life with engaging narration.

Sneak Peek into the Spookiness

Ghostly Giggling Guffaws:

Why are ghosts such bad liars?
You can see right through them.

Creepy Corny Cackles:

Why did the scarecrow win the Nobel Prize?
Because he was outstanding in his field.

Wicked Witchy One-Liners:

What did the witch say to her next victim (YOU!)?
Bewitch ya in a minute.

Why You WILL...you WILL...you WILL...Be Be-witched and Love
This Book

Entertaining & Engaging: Keeps everyone laughing &
entertained.

Great Gift Idea: Perfect for Halloween enthusiasts & joke lovers.

Boosts Creativity: Encourages storytelling & humor skills.

Don't Miss Out!

Embrace the Halloween spirit & add a dash of humor to your
festivities.

Whether you're trick-or-treating, hosting a party, or just love a
good laugh, this book is your go-to source for Halloween hilarity.

Get This Book Now & Make This Halloween the Funniest One
Yet!

Prepare for a monstrous amount of fun with every mysterious
turn of the page!

CHAPTERS/AUTHORS:

1. Ghosts & Apparitions

Misty Knight
G. Host
Phantom Writer
Spook E. Specter

2. Vampires & Dracula
Count Pun-ula & his cousin
Count Pen-ula
Dr. Acula
Bella Lugiggles

3. Zombies & the Undead
Anita Rest
Mort Tishen
Zed Deadman

4. Witches & Wizards
Wanda Spell
Albus Punbledore
Wizard of Ahhs

5. Werewolves & Shape-shifters
Warren Wolfe
Lycan B. Normal
Furrest Howlington

6. Monsters & Creatures
Frank N. Stein
Beastly Writerson
Mon Starr

7. Haunted Houses
Manor O. Fear
Haunt E. Mansion
Dwight N. Shining

8. Skeletons & Bones
Skel E. Ton
Anita Body
Cal C. Um

9. Mummies & Ancient Curses
Pharaoh Moans
Wrapsody Jones
Annie Tut

10. Pumpkins & Jack-o'-Lanterns
Jack O. Lantern
Gord N. Orange
Autumn Carver

11. Black Cats & Superstitions
Felix Omen
Kitty K. Lure
Whiskers McLuck

12. Graveyards & Tombstones
Phil Graves
Doug M. Deep
Hughes Mort Stone
…
All the way to:
20. Alien Encounters & UFOs
Al E. N.
Martian Wells
U.F. Owen

Ultimate Horror Trivia Quiz Book & Family Halloween Game: 666 Easy To Challenging Multiple-Choice Questions Of Spooky Scary Movies Monsters Gothic Romance Lit. Folklore & Legends From 1700S-Today

Unlock the Mysteries of Horror Across the Centuries!

Are you ready to delve into the darkest corners of horror history? Introducing the Ultimate Horror Trivia Challenge, a comprehensive quiz book that spans over three centuries of spine-chilling horror. From classic literature to modern films to gothic romance this collection is designed to thrill, educate & bring together fans of the genre from every generation.

Why This Book Is a Must-Have for Horror Enthusiasts, Couples & Families:

Extensive Content: 666 challenging multiple-choice questions covering a vast array of topics, including iconic horror films, legendary monsters, haunting literature & chilling folklore from the 1700s to today.

Multigenerational, Easy to Challenging Fun: Perfect for family game nights, gatherings, or sleepovers, this book bridges the generational gap. Whether you're a fan of classic horror novels or modern cinematic scares, there's something for everyone - even educators!

Educational and Entertaining: Test your knowledge & learn fascinating facts about the horror genre. Discover the stories behind legendary creatures, the inspiration for terrifying tales & the evolution of horror over the centuries.

Interactive Experience: Available in Ebook, paperback, hardcover & audiobook formats, you can read alone or engage with others. The audiobook version brings questions to life, making it ideal for road trips, parties, walks, workouts, or cozy romantic nights in: let the audio transform you into a contestant on a live horror trivia game show!

Perfect Gift: Looking for the ideal gift for the horror fan in your life? This comprehensive trivia collection is a unique & thoughtful present providing hours of entertainment.

What You'll Discover Inside:

Easy to seriously challenging questions about classic horror literature like Mary Shelley's Frankenstein & Bram Stoker's Dracula.

In-depth trivia on iconic horror films, from silent-era masterpieces to contemporary blockbusters.

Exploration of legendary monsters & folklore, including werewolves, vampires, ghosts, & more.

Questions that cover international horror, delving into tales & films from around the world.

3 BONUSES!:

1. Suggested Ways to Play & Rules to Enhance Your Horror Trivia Experience

2. Meta Horror Short True(?) Story by and about the Author

3. True Horror Story

Benefits of This Trivia Challenge:

Strengthen Family Bonds: Engage in friendly competition & spark conversations across generations. Share your favorite horror moments & discover new ones together.

Enhance Knowledge: Deepen your understanding of the horror genre's rich history & its impact on culture.

Versatile Use: Ideal for solo enthusiasts, couples, horror clubs, educators, & anyone looking to host an unforgettable horror trivia night.

Don't Miss Out on This Unique Horror Experience!

Whether you're a die-hard horror aficionado or new to the genre, this book offers an unparalleled journey through the world of horror. It's more than just a quiz book; it's a gateway to centuries of storytelling that have captivated & terrified audiences worldwide.

Get Your Copy Now & Play Today: Embark on a Thrilling Adventure Through Horror History!

Available Formats: Ebook/Paperback/Hardcover/Audiobook

Perfect For: Family Game Nights, Romantic Couples, Halloween/ Mardi Gras/Costume/Full Moon/Friday the 13th Parties, Horror Fans, Trivia Enthusiasts, Educators

Order now: test your courage & knowledge against the most comprehensive horror trivia collection ever assembled.

Dare to challenge yourself & others—if you think you can handle it!

Baby Boomers Trivia Quiz Book & Family Game - 331 Easy To Challenging Questions About Pop Culture: Nostalgic 50S 60S 70S 80S Movies, Music, Tv, Art, Fashion, Video Games, People...We All Love & Enjoy

Rediscover the Magic of the Past with the Ultimate Trivia Experience!

Do you ever find yourself reminiscing about the golden days: Elvis, Beatlemania, groovy 70s disco nights, 80s big hair & neon colors? Now you can relive all those cherished memories while this one-of-a-kind trivia quiz book takes you back in time, decade by decade!

Must Have for Every Baby Boomer & Your Whole Family - Grandparents to Grandchildren!:

331 Pop Culture Questions: Dive into extensive questions covering every aspect of the 50s to 80s. From unforgettable music & blockbuster movies to classic TV, iconic fashion trends, video games, & influential figures – this quiz book captures it all!

Perfect Multi-Generational, All Ages, Easy to Challenging Fun:

Fun & engaging for everyone by design – whether you're a Baby Boomer looking to test your memory or a knowledge-hungry (starved?) younger family member.

Nostalgic & Entertaining: Each question will take you on a sentimental journey down memory lane, sparking stories & laughter about the times you danced to "Stayin' Alive," watched "Dallas", or played your 1st arcade game.

Engage Family & Friends: This book is the perfect way to bond at family gatherings, road trips, or game nights. Set up teams, challenge each other, or enjoy a solo time trip back.

Ebook/audio/book Formats: Experience the convenience of Kindle or paperback/hardback for quick access anytime, anywhere, or immerse yourself in the audiobook quiz while driving, relaxing at home, or working out. The engaging narration brings each question to life & makes you feel like a live trivia game show contestant!

Re/Discover:

50s: Relive rock 'n' roll's birth, Hollywood glamour, iconic TV & fashion trends.

60s: Test your knowledge: British Invasion, Woodstock, groovy fashion, historic TV.

70s: Dance your way through disco fever, classic rock, bell-bottoms, birth of video games.

80s: Get ready for power ballads, big hair, neon fashion, classic arcade games, unforgettable "laugh out loud" sitcoms.

Who For?

Baby Boomers relive your youth & test your memory

Families looking for an entertaining, educational, multigenerational game to enjoy together

Trivia enthusiasts eager for a fresh challenge spanning four vibrant decades

Friends seeking a quick, easy, fun activity for game nights, barbecues, or holiday gatherings

Great Gift Idea!

Perfect birthday, holiday, or just-because gift? This book is a unique, thoughtful present of fun, laughter, memories: fantastic way to connect across generations & introduce younger folks to incredibly magical decades.

You'll Love:

✓ 331 Carefully Curated Questions
✓ Easy to Challenging Levels
✓ Fun for Individuals & Groups Quiz nights, family reunions, or parties!
✓ Bringing Back the Magic

Readers:

"A fantastic trip down memory lane! It brought back so many memories of my childhood and teen years."

"Perfect for family game night (grandparents!) even my kids loved learning about our 'old days'!'"

"As a trivia buff, I found this book to be well-organized, fun, & full of fascinating facts."

Ready to challenge your knowledge & relive the greatest decades of pop culture?

Don't miss out on this ultimate trivia experience!

Click "Buy Now" & let Baby Boomers Trivia Quiz Book & Family Game start your journey back in time – available now/soon in all formats!

Perfect for Baby Boomers, Gen X, Gen Y, Millennials, & anyone who loves fun!

Relive the magic, test your knowledge, bond with family & friends: Grab your copy today & let the fun begin!

In The Shadow Of A Giant - A Short Story: Sci-Fi Tale Of Noble Houses' Epic Starship Battles, Political Intrigue, Sabotage, Betrayal, Revenge And, Ultimately, Survival In A Decaying Galactic Empire

In the Shadow of a Giant invites readers on a pulse-pounding space epic, set in a universe where remnants of a collapsed empire battle for survival and supremacy in a lawless galaxy. In the vast, empty reaches of space, a fleet of merchant starships sails under the command of Commodore Gideon Adira, a man of noble lineage but dwindling resources. His convoy, carrying precious cargo to feed the crumbling Space City Albion, must navigate treacherous star lanes, where danger lurks behind every asteroid and enemies are never far from striking.

The giant looming in this tale is literal and metaphorical—a massive, decaying space city, once the heart of an empire, now a shadow of its former glory. Its inhabitants, billions strong, teeter on the brink of starvation, relying on the courage of men like Adira to bring them supplies and fend off the marauding pirate fleets that haunt the stars. But corruption and incompetence have crippled Albion, a place where noble houses, once bastions of power, have degenerated into feudal lords bickering over scraps of power.

Enter Commodore Gideon Adira, a man born to a noble house, yet scorned by the powerful due to his family's diminished status. Unlike other commanders who rule through fear, Gideon is a man of honor in a dishonorable world, and his crew follow him with a rare loyalty. They embark on a high-stakes journey, not just for survival, but to seize an opportunity that could elevate their fortunes—an asteroid cluster rich in resources, coveted by rival houses.

But as they venture beyond the relative safety of Albion's defenses, will they find themselves in the crosshairs of Ivan Morozov, a brutal enemy from a rival house? The Dominator, a fearsome warship under Morozov's command, sets its sights on Gideon's fleet. The tension rises as a high-stakes game of cat-and-mouse unfolds, and the stakes become life and death. Morozov's savagery knows no bounds—will he capture Adira or his loyal followers? Will the Adira line end?

Gideon Adira is not a man who backs down from a fight. Won't he - using his wits and the loyalty of his well-trained crew - concoct a daring plan to finally defeat the Dominator? Or will the mighty warship bear down on the Adira convoy, pummeling it with destructive energy lances? Will Gideon hold his nerve?

Will he wait for the perfect moment to strike? The Dominator seems unstoppable, a relic of the Old Empire's unstoppable might, unless...

Can Adira come up with a way to reduce the mighty ship to a drifting hulk? Will Gideon come up with a brilliant and brutal endgame and triumph over his enemy? Certainly not through sheer force, but with strategy and precision? Will he end Ivan Morozov's reign of terror in a blaze of destruction or will he and all his faithful followers perish?

Will his fleet ever make it back to Albion? Triumphant or bloodied or destroyed? The story gives readers the haunting fear that Adira's whole fleet will become a ghostly reminder of the perils and the power of this unforgiving universe. Or will underdog Gideon Adira ascend to new heights? The question lingers—how long can a man of honor survive in a galaxy so consumed by corruption and decay?

In the Shadow of a Giant is a gripping tale of honor, betrayal, and cunning warfare set against the backdrop of a galaxy in decline. Fans of space operas like Dune and The Expanse will find themselves enthralled by the intricate politics, the fierce battles, and the richly detailed world in which Gideon Adira fights not just for survival, but for a legacy. With pulse-pounding action, high-stakes drama, and a richly textured world teetering on the edge of chaos, this short story is a must-read for anyone who craves adventure among the stars.

The Last Stand Of The Golems - A Short Story: A Post-Apocalyptic Battle For Survival - Mechanical Golem Soldiers Vs. The Mortis Plague's Undead Hordes

What if the survival of the human race depended not on people, but on machines?

Humanity is an endangered species. Earth, once the cradle of life, is now a decaying wasteland overtaken by the unstoppable Mortis Plague. This ancient, incomprehensible force consumes all in its path, turning every living thing into part of its ever-growing army of the undead. Mankind's armies are shattered. Its will to fight is broken. Its last remaining hope lies in the fleet of interplanetary arks it has built, and the legions of mechanical golems set to defend them.

Many arks were destroyed before they could escape. Many more have launched, and are shoring up mankind's defenses on Luna or preparing an enclave to weather the storm on Mars. Only one ark ship, with thousands of lives aboard, has yet to leave its dying world. As the armies of the Plague close around it, many begin to doubt if it will leave at all.

All seems lost for the refugees on the ark. The last remnants of mankind's great army, a unit of veteran golems without the programming to feel fear, are all that stands between them and assimilation into the Plague's horrific legions. Their purpose is singular: to delay the enemy as long as possible and buy time to launch the ark.

As the countdown to launch ticks down and the golems are pushed back to the innermost barricades, the situation grows ever more desperate for the ark and its passengers. Will the captain's military brilliance, or timely aid from an unexpected source, save the ark from being overrun and joining its ruined brethren on the dead surface of Earth?

Buy this short story now - the first in a series that will make a saga - to find out!

Made in the USA
Monee, IL
27 October 2024

68769834R00164